BRITAIN'S LEGAL SYSTEMS

Contents

Introduction

Although Britain[1] is a unitary state it does not have a single legal system. Instead, England and Wales, Scotland, and Northern Ireland all have their own legal systems, with considerable differences in law, organisation and practice. This situation arises from the arrangements set in place when the different parts of the country were united. Since 1707 the existence of a single Parliament for England, Wales and Scotland and, in civil proceedings, of a common final court of appeal (the House of Lords), has resulted in substantial similarity on many points, while a large volume of modern legislation applies throughout Britain. Nevertheless considerable differences remain.

Britain's judiciary is a distinct organ of government alongside Parliament, which is the legislature (and the supreme authority), and the executive, which is headed by the Government. The judiciary is independent of both the legislature and the executive. It plays an important role in Britain's system of government by determining common law and interpreting statutes which together make up a large part of the constitution.[2]

This book, as part of the Aspects of Britain series, deals with the country's three legal systems separately. It describes their origins; the structure of the court systems; legal procedure—both civil

---

[1]The term 'Britain' is used in this book to mean the United Kingdom of Great Britain and Northern Ireland; 'Great Britain' comprises England, Wales and Scotland.

[2]For further details, see *The British System of Government* (Aspects of Britain: HMSO, 1992) and *Parliament* (Aspects of Britain: HMSO, 1991).

and criminal—and the administration of justice. The recent
Aspects of Britain title, *Criminal Justice* (HMSO, 1992), describes
the workings of the criminal justice system in greater detail and
contains sections on crime prevention measures and on the probation and prison services as well as covering recent reforms in the
criminal justice system. A further Aspects of Britain title, *Human
Rights*, examines the progress made in the application of the United
Nations' human rights covenants in Britain.

Although every attempt has been made to ensure that the
book is accurate and up-to-date, it should not be regarded as offer-
ing a definitive view on legal matters.

The Legal System of England and Wales

Origins of English Law

English law is the historical source of the Anglo-American or 'common law' group of legal systems. It is quite distinct from the Romano-Germanic or 'civilian' systems common in Western Europe and South America which derive from the law of the Roman Republic and Empire.

Roman law was codified in the sixth century by the Emperor Justinian but later fell into decay. It was revived with the renaissance of legal studies in European universities in the twelfth and thirteenth centuries.

The historic development of English law has been quite different from that of the Romano-Germanic systems and accounts for some of the differences between England and Wales and Scotland. In the period between the renaissance of Roman law studies at European universities and the codification of European national laws which began about 1800, the continental systems were dominated by the writings of jurists or legal writers who strongly influenced legal practice. In contrast, English courts evolved the law case by case, and English lawyers derived their law from the reports of the judges' decisions rather than from jurists' writings. The effects of these two different traditions are a matter for debate, but they are normally considered to have produced different kinds of legal systems and differences in legal approach and outlook.

The main sources of English law are: legislation, 'unwritten' law, and European Community law, as follows:

—*Legislation* consists of laws made by, or under the authority of, Parliament and may comprise *statutes* (Acts of Parliament) or *delegated legislation*. Delegated legislation comprises 'statutory instruments'—Orders in Council, orders, rules and regulations made by a government minister under the authority of a statute—and *by-laws* made by local government or other authorities exercising powers given to them by Parliament.

— *'Unwritten' law* consists of the common law and equity.

—*European Community law* (see p. 102), which arises from Britain's membership of the European Community, stands alongside both domestic legislation and the unwritten law, and, where there is any conflict, takes precedence over them.

Although there is at present no code of English law there has been a considerable amount of statutory codification of branches of the law in the form of Great Britain or United Kingdom statutes, especially in commercial law (concerning, for example, sale of goods, bills of exchange, consumer credit and partnership). The British technique of statutory codification results in codes which tend to be more detailed and narrower in scope than codes elsewhere in Western Europe. The law today is contained in about 3,500 Acts of Parliament, over 10,000 statutory instruments and statutory rules and orders, and countless reported cases.

England and Wales have a common legal system. The Acts of Union in 1536 and 1542 united England and Wales administratively, politically and legally.

Common Law

The common law of England evolved from the rules and practices of the community which were gradually formalised by decisions made by judges. The term 'common law' distinguished it from local laws, the canon laws of the Roman Catholic Church (which, until the Reformation in the sixteenth century, was the established church in England),[3] and the 'law merchant' practised in mercantile courts.

In the Anglo-Saxon period (from, roughly, the fifth to the eleventh century) the principles applied in the courts were based on the customs of the local community as declared by the freemen of those communities, who acted as judges. After the Norman Conquest in 1066, the King's judges gradually established a body of general principles based on the many local customs. These principles were applied uniformly during the judges' periodic circuits through the country and later at the royal courts in London—the courts of Common Pleas, King's Bench, and Exchequer.

Judicial Precedent

In order to achieve consistency, the judges placed great reliance on previous judgments given in similar cases. This practice has given rise to the doctrine of judicial precedent on which all law, other than legislation passed by Parliament, is based. Judges are bound to follow the decision of the courts above them in the hierarchy, and the appellate courts are generally bound to follow previous decisions at their own level. However, in 1966 the House of Lords declared that it would in future be prepared to depart from its past decisions where it seemed just to do so.

[3]For further details, see *Religion* (Aspects of Britain: HMSO, 1992).

It is likely that originally the necessary information on precedents was passed from one judge to another by personal contact. Towards the end of the thirteenth century the practice of noting down and circulating the rulings of judges (both on circuit and in the royal courts) developed. The arguments used by pleaders—as barristers (see p. 54) were then called—were also recorded. The notes were set out in Year Books covering the period 1283 to 1535; they were the forerunners of the published Law Reports that have existed in one form or another for more than 400 years.

Writs

Actions in the common law courts were initiated by writs obtained from the Chancery (the office of the Chancellor and a skilled body of clerks).[4] Writs were originally used by the Sovereign to settle disputes brought to his notice by subjects who considered themselves to have been wronged. They soon developed from a royal command ordering that an alleged wrong be put right, into a direction to an official to hold an inquiry into a complaint, or to a defendant either to concede or to answer a plaintiff's claim. During the twelfth and early thirteenth centuries a great many writs were issued in a wide variety of forms, and they began to shape the main branches of common law and the procedure appropriate to them. Eventually a semi-official register of writs appeared; this came to be regarded as a comprehensive catalogue of the causes of action known to law.

The framework of the writ system (together with a temporary restriction on the creation of new writs) slowed down the develop-

[4]The chief clerks were called masters. The foremost among them was known as the Master of the Rolls and frequently deputised for the chancellor.

ment of the common law. After 1285, litigants were again able to
obtain writs, but they ceased to be able to rely upon redress.

Equity

The medieval common law had a number of weaknesses. It did not
cover the whole field of legal obligations. It had no means of
extracting the truth from litigants, since it relied on documents and
refused to listen to the parties themselves. Its judgments could not
be adapted to special circumstances. It also lacked an ability to
implement its decisions—a successful legal suit could prove to be
an empty victory for the winning party.

Some people who failed to get satisfaction in the common law
courts were allowed to petition the Sovereign or his council. These
petitions were handled by the Chancellor who, as well as being
'Keeper of the King's Conscience', was head of the writ office. In
this capacity he was presumed to be acquainted with the general
working of the law. At first the Chancellor made recommendations
to the council, but soon he began to take decisions on his own. As a
result petitions came to be addressed directly to the Court of
Chancery rather than to the King. During the fifteenth century
these petitions became more frequent. By the sixteenth century
there were certain areas of law where it was usual for the Chancellor
to provide relief. In contrast to the common law, remedies in equity have remained discretionary.

In certain matters the Court of Chancery was able to enforce
rights not recognised at common law (those concerning trusts and
married women's property, for example). In other matters, such as
contract, fraud, accounts and partnerships, it was able either to
provide a more efficient alternative remedy or to provide a replace-
ment for a common law remedy which had been lost. In matters

outside its direct jurisdiction it could use its special procedure to achieve the following:

—to help to determine the rights of parties in other courts by forcing them to disclose facts and documents;[5]

—to secure for the plaintiff, if successful, the fruits of the legal victory; and

—to protect any third person from injury caused by the conflicting rights of others.

The Court of Chancery exercised an overriding jurisdiction. It could prevent proceedings in the common law courts from becoming an instrument of oppression either by restraining their commencement or prosecution, or by forbidding the enforcement of a judgment.

Thus equity, as exercised by the Court of Chancery, afforded an improved means of attaining justice, and this was the extent of the difference between equity and common law. However, no Chancellor ever attempted to dispute the right of common law judges to pronounce on the law. Gradually, under more conservative Chancellors, the Court of Chancery adopted the common law practice of relying on the process of legal analogy, and sought to apply the principle that 'equity follows the law'. As a result, by the end of the eighteenth century, equity had evolved into a body of legal doctrine as settled as the common law. Indeed the two systems were so similar—except that they dealt with different claims and provided different remedies—that there was little to choose between them in terms of simplicity and speed. By the nineteenth

[5]The reliance of the common law courts on written documents for most of their evidence rendered them powerless if the document required was in the hands of the opposing party, or contained a mistake, or was lost.

century equity rules had become so involved and technical that long delays were frequent; a dispute involving both common law and equity could take years to resolve.

Reforms were made in 1873 and 1875 by the Supreme Court of Judicature Acts. These reorganised the courts and provided that, in their new form, all should use and apply both common law and equity. The Act of 1873 laid it down that where rules of common law conflicted with those of equity the latter were to prevail.

Legislation

The earliest examples of enacted laws in England were the ordinances of the *Curia Regis* (the King and his council), the governing body of the realm in the early Norman period. Parliament did not begin to make law until the thirteenth century; by the sixteenth century legislative Acts took their present form.[6]

Until the late nineteenth century the amount of legislation was comparatively small but during the present century there has been a very great increase in the volume of legislation and its scope. Today almost all aspects of life are affected by the law.

Parliament is the supreme law-making body in Britain. Acts of Parliament are binding on all courts and take precedence over other sources of law. They are formal announcements of rules of conduct to be observed in the future and remain in force until they are repealed. Acts cannot be *ultra vires* ('outside the competence of'— in this case—Parliament).

Although the principles of natural justice (broadly, rules which an ordinary, reasonable person would consider fair) have

[6] 'Be it enacted by the Queen's most Excellent Majesty, by and with the advice and consent of the Lords Spiritual and Temporal, and Commons, in this present Parliament assembled, and by the authority of the same, as follows:–'. For further details, see *Parliament* (Aspects of Britain: HMSO, 1991).

always occupied an important position in the British constitution, they have never been codified in the form of guaranteed rights. Rights of personal freedom, such as the right of freedom of discussion and the rights of association and public meeting, could not be upheld by the courts if taken away by Act of Parliament. The courts are not entitled to question or even discuss the validity of Acts of Parliament. They are required only to interpret them according to the wording used or, if Parliament has failed to make its intentions clear, according to established rules of interpretation. If a court reaches a decision which is contrary to the intentions of Parliament, Parliament must either accept the decision or pass an amending Act; in the meantime the court's decision stands.

Under the traditional doctrine, in the event of conflict between two statutes, the later Act always prevails over the earlier one. Thus any Act passed by Parliament must be followed by the courts even though an earlier Act may have sought to prohibit the passing of such an Act.

Delegated Legislation

In order to reduce pressure on parliamentary time, much legislation gives ministers and other authorities the power to regulate administrative details by making 'delegated legislation'. In order to minimise the risk that powers given to the executive might undermine parliamentary government, they are normally delegated to authorities directly responsible to Parliament. These include government ministers, government departments for which ministers are responsible, or organisations whose regulations are subject to confirmation. Moreover, the Acts of Parliament concerned often provide for some measure of parliamentary control over the delegated legislation by giving Parliament the right to affirm or annul it. Certain Acts also state that the organisations affected must be consulted before rules and orders can be made.

The principle that the courts do not question the validity of parliamentary legislation does not apply to subordinate legislation. It is open to any court before which such legislation may come to decide whether it is *intra vires* (within its competence) or *ultra vires* (see p. 9).

Branches of the Law

The two main branches of the law in England and Wales are criminal law and civil law, a division which was established after the Norman conquest when a difference was first made between wrongs within the area of responsibility of the State—'pleas of the Crown'—and other wrongs. The distinction lies less in the nature of the acts and omissions covered by the two categories than in the nature of the subsequent legal proceedings and the hierarchy of law courts involved. The same wrongful act may often be both a crime and a civil wrong—for example, reckless or dangerous driving, a criminal offence, may also give rise to a civil action if it results in injury to, or damage to the property of, other people.

There is, as a rule, no reason why a criminal prosecution and a civil action should not both be brought, since proceedings are quite separate and independent, and take place before different courts. Broadly speaking, however, civil law relates to the rights, duties and obligations of individuals between themselves, whereas criminal law is concerned with wrongs affecting the community at large—acts contrary to the order, peace and well-being of society. Such acts render the offender liable to punishment by the state.

Other branches of the law are service law, administrative law, industrial law, Admiralty law and ecclesiastical law.

Criminal Law[7]

In most cases the criminal law recognises a particular intention or state of mind as a necessary part of a criminal offence (there are some cases of 'strict liability' where this is not necessary). However ignorance of the law on the part of an accused person is never accepted as an excuse. The law punishes not only criminal acts but also—as incitements, attempts or conspiracies—steps towards the commission of a crime which may never take place. People may be exempted from criminal liability because they have been deprived of their free will and self-control—by coercion or insanity, for instance. Some classes of people, such as children under ten years, may also be exempted from liability. Overseas diplomats in Britain may be entitled to immunity from criminal proceedings, but are expected to respect the law.

The classification of crimes is often based on the kind of harm done. There are crimes, for instance, against the person of the individual (such as assault or murder), against his or her property (burglary, arson and theft are examples), and against public rights which belong in common to all citizens (such as treason and offences against public order). Classification may also be based on the methods of 'trial' (as criminal proceedings are known). Serious crimes are usually tried 'upon indictment' (or formal accusation) before a judge and jury; less serious crimes are tried 'summarily' before magistrates sitting without a jury.

Civil Law

The main sub-divisions of civil law are:

—*family law,* which includes the laws governing marriage, divorce, and the custody of children;

[7]For further details, see *Criminal Justice* (Aspects of Britain: HMSO, 1992).

—the *law of property* (including intangibles, such as patents to inventions), which governs ownership and rights of enjoyment, the creation and administration of trusts, and the disposal of property on death;

—the *law of contract* which regulates, for instance, the sale of goods, loans, partnerships, insurance and guarantees; and

—the *law of torts*, which governs such actionable wrongs as negligence, defamation, malicious prosecution, nuisance and trespass—that is to say, injuries suffered by one person at the hands of another, irrespective of any contract between them.

Other Branches of the Law

Service law is codified in Acts of Parliament for the Royal Navy, the Army and the Royal Air Force (and in the delegated legislation made under the authority of those Acts). It is administered by courts martial and applies to all serving members of the armed forces of the Crown throughout the world and in some cases to their husbands and wives. Its purpose is to preserve discipline. No change of substantive law can be made except by Parliament. People subject to military law do not cease to be subject to the ordinary law. Their obligations as members of the armed forces are in addition to, and not instead of, their duties as citizens.

Administrative law is particularly concerned with the executive and judicial powers conferred by Parliament on the administration, and with their effect on the individual. The idea of rules of law which govern the relations of the governed and those governing them has existed for centuries. However it is only during the last 70 or so years, with the growth of state intervention in the life and activities of the subject, that it has been recognised as a separate branch of the law.

Industrial law is contained in a number of Acts of Parliament. It is concerned with conditions of employment, relations between employer and employees, and the legal position of trade unions, employers' associations and other organisations.

Admiralty law was originally concerned with crime, as well as with tort and contract upon the high seas. It is now limited to civil matters but, because it deals with cases involving foreign as well as British vessels, its rules differ from those which would apply in relation to the same matters on land.

Ecclesiastical law consists of elements of the old canon law which continued in force after the Reformation in the sixteenth century, together with the post-Reformation statutes and canons of the Church of England. These have been passed by Parliament, and are today passed by the General Synod of the Church of England, which under its previous title of the National Assembly was set up by Act of Parliament in 1919. It is the central legislative body of the Church and its measures are endorsed by Parliament.[8]

In the past, ecclesiastical law governed the clergy in all their affairs, and lay people in matters of faith and morals, including those aspects of their lives in which the ministrations of the Church were needed. By the beginning of the nineteenth century many of the offences recognised by the Church in the Middle Ages had become obsolete and others had become the subject of proceedings in the ordinary courts. Later in the nineteenth century the Church's jurisdiction in matrimonial matters and over personal property after death was transferred to newly established civil courts. Modern ecclesiastical law is thus concerned only with the regulation of church affairs, the discipline of the clergy in matters of doctrine and conduct, and control over church buildings and churchyards.

[8]For further details, see *Religion* (Aspects of Britain: HMSO, 1992).

Courts of Law

As a general rule, all court proceedings must be held in public—in what is known as 'open court'. However, in exceptional circumstances, the court may sit *in camera*—that is to say, when the press and the public may be excluded. These include cases where national security is involved; where the subject matter of the law suit is a secret industrial or commercial process; or where the proceedings relate to the wardship, custody and access, or adoption of an infant. The court's jurisdiction may also be exercised in private. In such cases judges and other judicial officers may transact certain kinds of business in chambers: only parties to the dispute and their legal advisers are admitted.

Nowadays courts can be created only by Act of Parliament. They may be classified in a number of ways. A distinction is sometimes made between *courts of record* and courts not of record. Those of record have an official record of the acts and judicial proceedings that have taken place there; they also have the power to fine and imprison for contempt of their authority. There is also a difference between *superior* and *inferior* courts—a superior court is one which is not subject to the control of any other court, except by way of appeal, and in which all matters are within its jurisdiction unless they are shown not to be so.

The most usual distinction is, however, between courts with criminal and those with civil jurisdiction. Even here, no hard and fast line can be drawn, as in certain circumstances civil cases are heard in criminal courts, while occasionally a criminal case may be heard in what is primarily a civil court.

In criminal cases the courts which first hear cases are the magistrates' courts and (for the more serious cases) the Crown Court.

In civil matters magistrates' courts have a limited jurisdiction, and the main courts are the county courts (for the lesser cases) and the High Court (where the more important cases are heard). The Court of Appeal in London, which has a Criminal Division and a Civil Division, hears appeals in criminal cases from the Crown Court and, in civil cases, from the county courts and the High Court. The Court of Appeal, the High Court and the Crown Court together form the Supreme Court of Justice. At the top of the hierarchy of courts is the House of Lords, which, in addition to being part of the legislature, is the final court of appeal in civil cases in the whole of Britain and, in criminal cases, for England, Wales and Northern Ireland.

Criminal Courts

Magistrates' Courts

A magistrates' court usually consists of a 'bench' of three lay, unpaid magistrates—known as justices of the peace ('JPs')—who are advised on points of law and procedure by a legally qualified clerk or a qualified assistant. There are nearly 28,000 lay magistrates serving some 450 courts. A few full-time, legally qualified stipendiary magistrates may sit alone; they usually preside in courts in urban areas where the workload is heavy. In 1992 there were 76 stipendiary magistrates in England and Wales.

Usually those charged with criminal offences first appear in a magistrates' court. Summary offences—the less serious offences which represent the vast majority of criminal cases—are tried by the magistrates themselves. The most serious offences, such as murder, manslaughter, rape and robbery, are tried on indictment (or formal accusation) only by the Crown Court. Usually those charged with such offences first appear before a magistrates' court, which decides whether to commit them to the Crown Court for trial. A third category of offences (such as theft, burglary or malicious wounding) are known as 'either way' offences; they can be tried either by magistrates or by jury in the Crown Court, depending on the circumstances of each case and the wishes of the defendant.

In cases of serious or complex fraud and in some cases involving child witnesses, committal proceedings in magistrates' courts may be bypassed at the discretion of the prosecution. However, the accused can apply to the Crown Court to be discharged on the ground that there is no case to answer.

Youth Courts

Cases involving people under 18 (in October 1992 this was raised from 17 under the provisions of the Criminal Justice Act 1991) are heard in youth courts (formerly juvenile courts). These are specialist magistrates' courts which either sit apart from other courts or are held at a different time. There are restrictions on public access and media coverage.

Where a person under 18 is charged jointly with someone of 18 or over, the case is heard in an ordinary magistrates' court or the Crown Court. If the young person is found guilty the court may transfer the case to a youth court unless satisfied that it is undesirable to do so.

The Crown Court

The Crown Court sits at about 90 centres and is presided over by High Court judges, full-time 'circuit judges' and part-time recorders. England and Wales are divided into six circuits for the purpose of hearing criminal cases. Each circuit is divided into areas containing one or more centres of the High Court and Crown Court. The six circuits are: Midland and Oxford, North-Eastern, Northern, South-Eastern (including London), Wales and Chester, and Western.

The Crown Court tries the most serious offences and 'either way' offences referred to it by magistrates (see above). All contested cases are presided over by a judge sitting with a jury.

Cases received from the magistrates' court as committals for trial form the largest element of the Crown Court's workload. In 1990, 103,011 cases were received for trial in the Crown Court, representing a four per cent increase on the numbers in 1989 and almost double the level received in 1980 (55,594).

Appeals

A person convicted by a magistrates' court may appeal to the Crown Court against sentence if he or she has pleaded guilty. The appeal may be made against both conviction and sentence if a not guilty plea has been made. The Divisional Court of the Queen's Bench Division of the High Court hears appeals on points of law and procedure—by either prosecution or defence—in cases originally dealt with by magistrates.

If convicted by the Crown Court, the defendant can appeal to the Court of Appeal (Criminal Division) against both conviction and sentence.

The House of Lords is the final appeal court, but it will only consider cases that involve a point of law of general public importance.

The Attorney General may seek the opinion of the Court of Appeal on a point of law which has arisen in a case where a person tried on indictment is acquitted. The Court has the power to refer the point to the House of Lords if necessary. The acquittal in the original case is not affected.

The Attorney General may also refer a case to the Court of Appeal if he or she considers that a sentence passed by the Crown Court is unduly lenient. This is restricted to cases which can only be tried in a Crown Court. If the Court of Appeal agrees, it may increase the sentence within the statutory maximum laid down by Parliament for the offence.

The Home Secretary may consider representations and intervene in cases where appeal rights have been exhausted. Fresh evidence is necessary if such action is to be taken.

Civil Courts

Magistrates' Courts
Magistrates' courts have limited civil jurisdiction which extends to family proceedings for custody and maintenance orders; adoption orders; guardianship orders; and family protection orders. The courts also have jurisdiction over public health cases and the recovery of local taxes. Committees of magistrates exercise semi-administrative functions in relation to the licensing of public houses and betting shops and clubs.

County Courts
The 274 county courts are located so that no part of England and Wales is an unreasonable distance from one of them. Their locations are not necessarily connected with the boundaries of administrative counties. In the busier centres they may sit every weekday: elsewhere they may sit weekly, monthly or at longer intervals. All

judges of the Supreme Court and all circuit judges and recorders have the power to sit in the county courts, but each court has one or more circuit judges assigned to it by the Lord Chancellor; regular sittings are normally taken by them. Every court has a district judge who deals with procedural matters and the various steps that have to be taken before an action is tried. The district judge also has jurisdiction to try cases up to £5,000 in value. As well as trying the larger actions the circuit judge hears appeals from decisions by the district judge.

The jurisdiction of county courts includes:

—actions founded upon contract and tort (see p. 13);

—trust and mortgage cases;

—action for the recovery of land;

—insolvency;

—cases involving disputes between landlords and tenants;

—complaints about race and sex discrimination;

—Admiralty cases and patent cases; and

—adoption, child care and divorce cases.

Some specialist work (patent cases, for example) is concentrated in certain designated courts. Since 1991 financial limits to the jurisdiction of county courts have been replaced, for non-specialist cases, with more flexible criteria relating to the substance, importance and complexity of cases. However, all personal injury claims worth up to £50,000 must be started in a county court, although the new criteria determine whether the case will be tried in a county court or in the High Court.

There are special arbitration facilities and simplified procedures for small claims not exceeding £1,000. In such cases, the district judge normally acts as arbitrator. He or she may take an active part in the proceedings, asking questions to discover the facts at issue and dispensing with strict rules of procedure and evidence. Legal representation is discouraged by providing that for claims of up to £1,000 in value, no legal costs can be recovered unless one of the parties has acted unreasonably. However, since October 1992, all restrictions have been removed from rights of audience in small claims proceedings, enabling lay representatives to appear on behalf of litigants.

The majority of the cases brought under the arbitration scheme concern goods sold and delivered, work done, or material supplied.

The High Court

The High Court deals with the more complicated civil cases (it also covers some criminal cases) as well as dealing with appeals from tribunals and from magistrates' courts in both civil and criminal matters. It has three divisions. Although the divisions do not have exclusive jurisdiction in any particular matter, in practice the jurisdiction is separate. Similarly the judges can sit in any division but in practice they specialise in the work of a particular division.

The *Family Division* is concerned with jurisdiction affecting the family, including that relating to wardship and adoption.

The *Chancery Division* deals with the interpretation of wills and the administration of estates, partnerships, mortgages, and the execution of trusts and settlements. The Division also deals with the 'revenue list' which consists mainly of income tax cases (these are always taken by a judge who has detailed knowledge of the subject); with the special law affecting companies (including their winding-up); and with some bankruptcy matters when they have been dealt with in the county courts.

Most other civil litigation comes before the *Queen's Bench Division*, which has a wide and varied jurisdiction, including contract and tort cases. Specialisation within this division is recognised to some extent in the placing of particular cases on different lists. Commercial cases are, for example, placed on the 'commercial list' and are heard by one of the two or three judges of the division with special experience of this type of litigation. Admiralty and 'prize' jurisdiction (dealing with naval matters and claims over captured ships or aircraft) is dealt with by a specially constituted Admiralty court within the Queen's Bench Division.

The *Lord Chief Justice* presides over the Queen's Bench Division.

The Lord Chancellor is the nominal president of the Chancery Division; in practice, he never attends and the administration of the division is the responsibility of the senior judge, known as the *Vice-Chancellor*. The Family Division has its own President. The maximum number of other ('puisne') High Court judges is 85. In September 1992 there were 53–83 in the Queen's Bench Division, 14 in the Chancery Division (including the Vice-Chancellor), and 16 in the Family Division.

When hearing cases in the first instance, High Court judges sit alone. Appeals in civil matters from inferior courts are dealt with by Divisional Courts of two (or sometimes three) judges, or by single judges of the appropriate division nominated by the Lord Chancellor. For example, appeals from the county courts in bankruptcy cases are heard by a Divisional Court of the Chancery Division; appeals on points of law from magistrates' courts come before Divisional Courts of the Queen's Bench Division; appeals against the decisions of the magistrates' courts in matrimonial proceedings lie to a Divisional Court of the Family Division.

The High Court sits in London at the Royal Courts of Justice (the 'Law Courts'). At 'first-tier' provincial centres, High Court judges hear civil cases as well as dealing with serious criminal cases.

In London the High Court has four sittings:

— *Michaelmas*, which normally begins on 1 October and ends on 21 December;

— *Hilary*, which begins on 11 January and ends on the Wednesday before Easter;

— *Easter*, which begins on the second Tuesday after Easter and ends on the Friday before the Spring Bank Holiday (usually the last Monday in May); and

— *Trinity*, which begins on the second Tuesday after the spring holiday and ends on 31 July.

Two judges are selected at the beginning of each Long Vacation (during the summer) to hear cases needing prompt attention.

Where the jurisdictions of the High Court and the county courts overlap, cases of exceptional importance, complexity or financial substance are reserved for trial in the High Court.

Appeals

Appeals in matrimonial, adoption and guardianship cases, and child care cases, which have been heard by magistrates' courts, go to the Family Division of the High Court (see above). Appeals from the High Court and county courts are heard in the Court of Appeal (Civil Division), and may go on to the House of Lords, the final national court of appeal in civil and criminal cases.

The Court of Appeal has several ex officio members: the Lord Chancellor, ex-Lord Chancellors, Lords of Appeal in Ordinary, the Lord Chief Justice, the Master of the Rolls and the President of the Family Division of the High Court. Of these members, only the Master of the Rolls normally sits in court. The ordinary judges are 16 Lords Justices of Appeal.

The court usually sits with a bench of three judges, except in 'interlocutory' matters (questions arising during the course of a case but before the actual hearing) when two judges may sit. In a very limited class of matters, not involving the final determination of an appeal, one judge sitting alone may make a decision. In ordinary cases each member of the court delivers a judgment, and the majority opinion prevails. On coming to a decision, the court has the power to order a new trial or the reversal or variation of a judgment.

The judges in the House of Lords usually sit as a group of five. Lay peers do not attend the hearings of appeals, which normally take place in a committee room, but peers who hold or have held high judicial office may also sit. The Lord Chancellor is President of the House in its judicial capacity.

Juries

Juries have been part of the legal system in England since at least the twelfth century. Trial by jury is not, however, the form of trial used in most courts. It has never been used in magistrates' courts; it is extremely rare in county courts; and it is used less and less in civil cases in the High Court. The principle of jury trial has been continuously maintained only in more serious criminal cases.

In jury trials the jury is responsible for deciding whether a defendant is 'guilty' or 'not guilty'—the latter verdict results in acquittal. The jury consists of twelve people, except in county courts where it consists of eight, and in coroners' courts (see p. 27), where it consists of from seven to eleven. If the jury is unable to reach a unanimous verdict, the judge may direct it to bring in a majority verdict if, in the normal jury of twelve people, no more than two disagree. In civil actions tried by jury, the jury is responsible not only for deciding questions of fact but also for fixing the amount of damages to be awarded to the injured party; in this case unanimity is necessary.

A jury is independent of the judiciary. Any attempt to interfere with a jury once it is sworn in is a criminal offence. Potential jurors are randomly selected for a panel before the start of the trial and a random selection is made from that panel for each case: the prosecution and the defence may challenge individual jurors who have been selected to try that case, giving reasons for doing so.

With certain exceptions, all people between the ages of 18 and 70 whose names appear on the electoral register are liable for jury service. Their names are chosen at random. Those who are ineligible include judges; people who have within the previous ten years been members of the legal profession or the police, prison or probation services; the clergy; and people suffering from mental illness. Anyone who has received a prison sentence of five years or more is disqualified for life from serving on a jury. People who have received sentences of less than five years, or have been placed on probation, are also disqualified for a period. Some people may claim 'excusal as of right' if called, including people over 65, Members of Parliament, serving members of the armed forces and people belonging to the medical and similar professions. Courts may also excuse those whose physical disabilities or lack of knowledge of the English language makes their ability to act as jurors doubtful.

People called for jury service are entitled to receive travelling expenses, together with a subsistence allowance. A financial loss allowance is payable to people who actually lose earnings or national insurance benefit as a result of jury service, up to a maximum of £41.40 a day for the first ten days' continuous service and up to £77.00 a day thereafter.

The Contempt of Court Act 1981 makes it an offence to obtain, disclose, solicit or publish details of a jury's deliberations.

The Judicial Committee of the Privy Council

The Judicial Committee of the Privy Council[9] derives its appellate jurisdiction from the traditional right of all the Queen's subjects to appeal for redress to the Sovereign in Council if they believe that the courts of law have failed to do them justice. It is now the final court of appeal from the courts of the British dependencies and from the courts of some independent members of the Commonwealth (including some in which the Queen is not Sovereign) who have not decided to discontinue the appeal. The Judicial Committee is also the final court of appeal from the Channel Islands and the Isle of Man. (The islands are Crown dependencies and are not part of Britain.) It is also the final court of appeal from the prize courts in Britain and its dependencies and from certain professional disciplinary committees. It has jurisdiction in a limited class of ecclesiastical appeals.

Appeals come to the Judicial Committee either where a right of appeal has been specially created—for instance, by statute, Order in Council or Letters Patent—or by special leave of the Sovereign in Council on the advice of the Judicial Committee. Appeals are heard by a board of the committee, whose members are usually selected from the Lord Chancellor, ex-Lord Chancellors

[9]For further details, see *The British System of Government* (Aspects of Britain: HMSO, 1992).

and Lords of Appeal in Ordinary. Lords Justices of Appeal and other members of the Privy Council who have held high judicial office (including Chief Justices and certain other judges from other Commonwealth countries who are not members of the Privy Council) may be asked to sit from time to time. In theory the Judicial Committee does not deliver judgment. It advises the Sovereign, who acts on its report and approves an Order in Council to give it effect. Its decisions, though not binding on the English courts, are treated with great respect.

Special Courts

In addition to the courts which exercise ordinary civil and criminal jurisdiction, there are a number of courts in England and Wales with special functions of various kinds. Some of these—for instance, coroners' courts, courts martial and ecclesiastical courts—are ancient courts modified to meet the needs of modern society. A greater number are comparatively new creations, set up by Act of Parliament to deal with the many problems arising from the State's regulation of the day-to-day affairs of the community.

Coroners' Courts

Coroners were first appointed in each county in the twelfth century to protect the fiscal rights of the Crown. From the beginning, coroners were concerned with violent and unexplained deaths, since in the past these brought revenue to the Sovereign through fines and the forfeiture of a convicted person's goods.

Today, coroners in England and Wales investigate violent and unnatural deaths or sudden deaths where the cause is unknown. However, an inquest is not necessary if a sudden death was due to natural causes; instead the coroner may order a post-mortem examination to determine the cause of death. The coroner must hold an inquest if the person died a violent or unnatural death or died in prison or in other specified circumstances. It is the duty of the coroner's court to establish how, when and where the person died. A coroner may sit alone or, in certain circumstances, with a jury. If the coroner has reason to suspect murder, suicide, manslaughter or infanticide, or that the death was caused by a road accident, he or she must summon a jury.

Courts Martial

Courts martial have jurisdiction over members of the armed forces and, in certain circumstances, their dependants and civilians employed by the armed forces who accompany them outside Britain. The courts do not have the power to deal with the offences of treason, murder, manslaughter, felony or rape committed by members of the services in Britain. In practice, non-military criminal offences committed by servicemen and servicewomen in Britain are normally dealt with in the ordinary courts.

Courts martial (which consist of a president and a number of serving officers) are convened by authorised officers. A judge advocate is appointed to sit with the court at all Royal Navy trials and in more serious Army and Air Force cases. He or she is responsible for advising on law and procedure and may sum up the evidence. The judge advocate in the case of the Army and the Air Force is normally a member of the judicial staff of the Judge Advocate General of the Forces, a civilian department responsible to the Lord Chancellor. Members of the staff must be barristers of at least five years' standing. In the case of the Navy, the judge advocate is a legally qualified serving officer.

People convicted by court martial may petition the military authorities responsible for confirming or reviewing the finding and sentence of the court martial. They can also appeal to the *Courts Martial Appeal Court*. Further appeal to the House of Lords is possible if the Courts Martial Appeal Court certifies that a point of general public importance is involved and it is considered that the point is one that ought to be ruled upon by the House. Servicemen and servicewomen can appeal to the Courts Martial Appeal Court only against finding. Civilians, however, in addition to their general right to petition a confirming or reviewing authority, can also appeal to the Courts Martial Appeal Court against sentence.

Ecclesiastical Courts

Since the constitution and law of the established Church of England are part of the public law of the country, the ecclesiastical courts are the Queen's courts. They have the status of public courts which have, within their own limited sphere, exclusive jurisdiction. The basis of the ecclesiastical court system is the court of the diocese, known as the *consistory court*, over which the Chancellor of the Diocese usually presides. (The Chancellor is a barrister appointed by the bishop, but possessing in his or her own right the authority of a judge of the Queen's court.) Above the consistory courts are the *provincial courts* of Canterbury and York. They are presided over by the same judge who is appointed jointly by the two archbishops. At the head of the system is the Judicial Committee of the Privy Council (see p. 26), which is assisted in ecclesiastical matters by a number of bishops summoned to attend as assessors.

Tribunals

Tribunals are a specialised group of judicial bodies, with some of the characteristics of courts of law. The growth in the number of tribunals reflects the expansion in government involvement in economic and social affairs: there are now over 2,000 tribunals dealing with over 1 million cases a year. They include tribunals concerned with land and property, national insurance and supplementary benefits, the National Health Service, industry and employment, immigration, transport and taxation.

Tribunals are normally set up under statutory powers which also govern their constitution, functions and procedure. Tribunals often consist of laypeople, but they are often chaired by someone who is legally qualified. They tend to be less expensive, and less formal, than courts of law. Independently of the executive, tribunals decide the rights and obligations of private citizens, and of government departments and local authorities. In the case of some tribunals, a two-tier system operates, with an initial right of appeal to a lower tribunal and a further right of appeal, at least on a point of law, to a higher tribunal and thence, usually, to the Court of Appeal. Appeals from single-tier tribunals usually lie to the High Court in England and Wales, to the Court of Session in Scotland, and to the Court of Appeal in Northern Ireland. There are a few exceptions including, for example, immigration appeals, where there is no right of appeal directly from the Immigration Appeals Tribunal to the courts. Even where there is no right of appeal to a court of law, an aggrieved person may challenge the decision by seeking leave to make an application for judicial review (see p. 45).

Tribunals usually consist of an uneven number of people so that a majority decision can be reached. Members are normally appointed by the government minister concerned with the subject, although in some cases where a lawyer is required to chair or serve as a member of the tribunal other authorities such as the Crown or Lord Chancellor have the power of appointment. Tribunals do not normally employ staff or spend money themselves, but their expenses are paid by the government departments concerned.

An independent advisory body known as the Council on Tribunals (appointed jointly by the Lord Chancellor and the Lord Advocate) exercises general supervision over the procedures and working of most tribunals, and reports on particular matters. (A Scottish Committee of the Council exercises the same function in Scotland.)

Restrictive Practices Court

The Restrictive Practices Court is an exception to the British system of courts of fairly general jurisdiction. It deals with matters relating to monopolies, restrictive trade practices and resale price maintenance. It comprises five judges from the three law districts of Britain—three from the English High Court, one from the Scottish Court of Session and one from the Northern Ireland Supreme Court—and up to ten other people appointed, on the recommendation of the Lord Chancellor, because of their experience and expertise in industry, commerce or public life. The quorum is three, of whom one must be a judge.

Procedure

Criminal Cases

Arrest

People may be arrested on a warrant issued by a magistrate on sworn information laid before him or her, or, in the case of 'arrestable' offences, without a warrant. If the person is charged with an offence he or she may be released on bail to attend a magistrates' court. When bail is not granted by the police the defendant must be brought before a magistrates' court as soon as possible. Although all those accused of offences have a general right to bail, magistrates may withhold bail on certain well defined grounds. If bail is refused by the magistrates, the defendant is entitled to apply to the Crown Court or the High Court judge in chambers and must be informed of this right. The Government is considering a number of changes to existing procedures.

Prosecution

Once the police have charged a person with a criminal offence, the *Crown Prosecution Service* assumes control of the case and independently reviews the evidence to decide whether to prosecute. Although the decision to prosecute is generally delegated to the lawyers in the area offices, some especially sensitive or complex cases are dealt with by the headquarters of the Service; these include terrorist offences and breaches of the Official Secrets Acts.[10]

Habeas Corpus

People detained in custody who think that the grounds for their detention are not lawful may apply for a writ of *habeas corpus* (a writ requiring a person to be brought before a court to investigate the lawfulness of his or her restraint) against the person who detained them. The person responsible must appear in court on a day named to justify the detention. (Lawful grounds are in pursuance of criminal justice; for contempt of court or of either House of Parliament; detention of persons found to be mentally disordered; detention of children by their parents or guardians; and detention expressly authorised by Act of Parliament.)

[10]For further details, see *Criminal Justice* (Aspects of Britain: HMSO, 1992).

The writ of *habeas corpus* applies in both civil and criminal cases. An application for such a writ is normally made to a divisional court of the High Court, either by the person detained or by someone acting on his or her behalf. If no court is sitting, application may be made to a single judge, who may, and in some cases must, direct that it should come before a divisional court. An application on behalf of anyone under 18 is first made to a judge sitting in chambers or in private. A writ may be refused only by a divisional court.

Trial

The trial has two parties: the prosecution and the defence. Since the law presumes that an accused person is innocent until proved guilty, the prosecution is not granted any advantage over the defence.

An accused person has the right to employ a legal adviser and may be granted legal aid from public funds (see p. 58). If remanded in custody, the accused person may be visited by a legal adviser to ensure a properly prepared defence.

The prosecution has a duty to disclose information to the defence by, for example, informing the defence of witnesses whose evidence may help the accused and whom the prosecution does not propose to call.

Criminal trials are normally held in open court and rules of evidence, which are concerned with the proof of facts, are rigorously applied. If evidence is improperly admitted, a conviction can be quashed on appeal. For instance, the evidence of one uncorroborated witness is generally sufficient. However, if the evidence is that of an accomplice (or accomplices) the judge will warn the jury of the danger of convicting on such uncorroborated evidence, and a conviction made without any such warning would not be upheld on appeal.

The defence or prosecution may suggest that the defendant's mental state renders him or her unfit to be tried. If the jury decides that this is so, the defendant may be admitted to a hospital specified by the Home Secretary.

During the trial the defendant has the right to hear and cross-examine witnesses for the prosecution, normally through a lawyer. He or she can call his or her own witnesses who, if they will not attend voluntarily, may be legally compelled to do so. The defendant can also address the court in person or through a lawyer, the defence having the right to the last speech at the trial before the judge sums up. The defendant cannot be questioned without consenting to be sworn as a witness in his or her own defence. When the defendant does testify, he or she may be cross-examined about character or other conduct only in exceptional circumstances; generally the prosecution may not introduce such evidence.

In criminal trials by jury the judge determines questions of law, sums up the evidence for the benefit of the jury, and acquits the accused or passes sentence according to the verdict of the jury. The jury alone, however, decides the issue of guilt or innocence. Verdicts need not necessarily be unanimous. In certain circumstances the jury may bring in a majority verdict provided that, in the normal jury of 12 people, not more than two dissent.

If the jury acquits the defendant, the prosecution has no right of appeal and the defendant cannot be tried again for the same offence. The defendant, however, has a right of appeal to the appropriate court if found guilty.

Extradition
Britain has extradition arrangements with 47 Commonwealth countries, with 19 countries under the European Convention on

Extradition, and with 27 foreign countries by bilateral treaty, although some of the treaties are not currently operative. Britain also has extradition arrangements with the Irish Republic. Limited extradition arrangements exist with other countries. Safeguards and rights of appeal are set out in the Extradition Act 1989.

Civil Proceedings

Civil proceedings are started by the aggrieved person; no preliminary inquiry is required. Actions in the High Court are usually begun by a writ served on the defendant by the plaintiff, stating the nature of the claim and the remedy sought. If the defendant intends to contest the claim, he or she 'enters an appearance' by informing the court to this effect. Before the case is set down for trial in the High Court, documents (pleadings) normally drafted by counsel and setting out the scope of the dispute, are filed with the court. The pleadings are also served on the parties involved. County court proceedings are initiated by a summons usually served on the defendant by the court.

In order to encourage parties to restrict the issues in dispute, the High Court and county courts have the power in most cases to order the pre-trial exchange of witness statements. Courts may impose penalties in costs on parties who unreasonably refuse to admit facts or disclose documents before trial.

Civil proceedings, as a private matter, can usually be abandoned or ended by settlement between the parties at any time. In most cases, parties to a dispute are able to settle their differences through their solicitors before the trial stage is reached. Actions brought to court are usually tried without a jury, except in cases of defamation, false imprisonment, or malicious prosecution or where fraud is alleged, when either party may apply for trial by jury. The jury decides questions of fact and determines damages to be paid to the injured party; majority verdicts may be accepted. The Court of Appeal may increase or reduce damages awarded by a jury if it considers them inadequate or excessive.

In divorce proceedings, a *decree nisi* must be pronounced in open court, but a procedure for most undefended cases dispenses with the need to give evidence in court and permits written evidence to be considered by the district judge.

Judgments in civil cases are enforceable through the authority of the court. Most of them are for payment of sums of money, and these may ultimately be enforced by seizure of the defendant's goods. A judgment may also be enforced by attachment of earnings—that is, by an order of a court (usually a county court)—requiring an employer to make periodic payments to the court from the defendant's wages. A judgment for the possession of land is enforced by an officer of the court putting the plaintiff in possession. Refusal to obey a judgment directing the defendant to do something or to abstain from doing something may result in imprisonment for contempt of court.

The general rule is that the costs of action (including the barrister's fees, the solicitor's charges and court fees) are in the discretion of the court, but normally the court orders the costs to be paid by the party losing the action.

In civil cases heard by a *magistrates' court*, the court issues a summons to the defendant setting out details of the complaint and the date on which it will be heard. Parties and witnesses give their evidence at the court hearing. Domestic proceedings are normally heard by not more than three lay justices, including, where practicable, a woman. Members of the public are not allowed to be present. The court may order provision for custody, access and supervision of children, as well as maintenance payments for husbands and wives and children. (From April 1993 a Child Support Agency will take over from the courts the main responsibility for child maintenance cases.)

The law has been changed recently to speed up civil proceedings in magistrates' courts by allowing written statements, expert opinions and hearsay evidence to be accepted in court without the presence of the witness, unless the evidence is disputed and the disputing party requests the presence of the witness.

The Courts and Legal Services Act 1990

The Courts and Legal Services Act 1990 makes significant changes in the English legal system. Among other things, the Act provides for the reallocation of civil law business, matching it more appropriately to the level of the court. It provides for the removal of all restrictions on the right of audience in certain county court proceedings thus enabling lay representatives to appear on behalf of litigants. It enables further procedural changes to be introduced which will speed up the progress of cases and cut costs. The jurisdiction of the Parliamentary Commissioner for Administration (the Ombudsman) has been extended to include the investigation of complaints of maladministration by court staff.

Brussels Convention on Civil Jurisdiction and Enforcement of Judgments

In 1987 Britain ratified the Brussels Convention on Civil Jurisdiction and Enforcement of Judgments. This unifies the rules of jurisdiction in the 12 European Community member states over a wide range of civil proceedings. The Convention's main rule is that defendants domiciled in a contracting state should be sued in that state. Each of the three British legal jurisdictions is treated as a separate state for this purpose. According to the principle of the 'free movement of judgments', foreign judgments are given the same treatment as domestic judgments for domestic purposes.

The Citizen's Charter

The Citizen's Charter, a government White Paper published in July 1991, sets out a number of proposals intended to raise quality, increase choice, secure better value, and extend accountability in public services. It includes a number of proposals intended to improve the working of the legal system.

A Courts Charter, one of a number of individual charters prepared under the Citizen's Charter initiative, was published in November 1992. It sets standards for those areas which concern users, such as privacy, the need for more information when people come to court, and the provision of waiting areas and refreshments. An independent inspectorate will be set up to monitor standards. The Charter also covers the conduct of court business, and guideline time limits will be set covering, among other things, the period between the start of proceedings and the first appearance in court.

The Charter will not cover judicial decisions.

A video explaining court procedures to jurors has been shown in most Crown court centres since July 1992. In order to meet the need for privacy in courts, special interview rooms are being provided in children's and family cases where possible. Where accommodation allows, separate waiting rooms are provided for witnesses who are victims of crime. Link officers are to be appointed in county courts to liaise between the court and advice agencies such as housing centres and Citizens' Advice Bureaux.

Action already taken to improve services to the public includes:

—the issue of an explanatory leaflet telling witnesses what to expect when they go to court;

—carrying out a range of surveys covering magistrates' courts, crown courts and county courts with the aim of improving services to the public;

—the display of notices in all court buildings outlining complaints procedures;

—the introduction of name badges for court staff dealing with the public; and

—the purchase of collapsible ramps for each crown court centre in order to ease the access of disabled people to jury boxes.

Administration of the Law

The administration of justice is the responsibility of the Lord Chancellor, the Home Secretary and the Attorney General. The highest judicial appointments are made by the Queen on the advice of the Prime Minister. The judiciary is independent and its adjudications are not subject to ministerial direction or control. There is no ministry of justice.

The Lord Chancellor

The Lord Chancellor, whose office probably dates back 1,400 years, is head of the judiciary. He or she is a senior Cabinet Minister, changing with the Government. The Lord Chancellor is concerned with court procedure and is responsible for the administration of all courts including, since April 1992, the magistrates' courts (formerly the responsibility of the Home Secretary). The Lord Chancellor is also responsible for a number of administrative tribunals. He or she recommends all other judicial appointments to the Crown and appoints magistrates. He or she has general responsibility for the legal aid and advice schemes and for the administration of civil law reform.

The Lord Chancellor's Office is a government department staffed by civil servants. A Parliamentary Under-Secretary of State, a junior minister, is answerable to the House of Commons.

In February 1992 the Government published the White Paper *A New Framework for Local Justice* which set out proposals intended to apply the principles of the Citizen's Charter (see p. 38) in order to provide a better service to the community and court users.

The Home Secretary

The Home Secretary, who is also a senior Cabinet minister, is concerned with the criminal law, the police service, prisons, and the probation and after-care service. He or she approves the appointment of justices' clerks. The Home Secretary appoints a board of visitors to each prison establishment and is advised by the Parole Board on the release of prisoners on licence.

The Home Secretary is also responsible for advising the Queen on the exercise of the royal prerogative of mercy to pardon a person convicted of a crime or to remit all or part of a penalty imposed by a court. These powers are normally used only where new facts or circumstances have come to light of which the courts were unable to take account when they dealt with the case.

Attorney General and Solicitor General

The Attorney General and the Solicitor General, known as the Law Officers of the Crown for England and Wales, are the Government's principal advisers on English law, and they represent the Crown in appropriate domestic and international cases, including cases at the European Court of Human Rights at Strasbourg and the International Court at The Hague. They are senior barristers, elected members of the House of Commons, and hold ministerial posts. As well as exercising various civil law functions, the Attorney General is responsible for the main prosecuting authorities.

In civil law matters the Attorney General can initiate proceedings in the High Court for the enforcement of public rights and on behalf of the interests of charity. He or she may appear as an independent state officer before judicial tribunals of inquiry.

The Solicitor General is, in effect, the deputy of the Attorney General. As head of the Crown Prosecution Service, the Director of Public Prosecutions is subject to superintendence by the Attorney General, as is the Director of the Serious Fraud Office.

Other Departments

The Treasury Solicitor provides a legal service for a large number of government departments in England and Wales. The duties of the Department of the Procurator General and Treasury Solicitor include:

— instructing Parliamentary Counsel (see below) on Bills and drafting subordinate legislation;

— representing other departments in court;

—giving general advice on the interpretation and application of the law;

—conveyancing of property;

—administration of residuary estates (estates undisposed of by will) of certain deceased people; and

—dealing with the outstanding property and rights of dissolved companies.

Some departments are wholly dependent on the Treasury Solicitor for their legal work. Some have their own legal staff for a proportion of the work, and draw on the Treasury Solicitor for special advice and, often, for litigation and conveyancing. Others, whose administrative work is based on, or deals with, a code of specialised law or involves a great deal of legal work, have their own independent legal sections.

The Treasury Solicitor is also the *Queen's Proctor* (an officer who has certain functions relating to the divorce laws).

The Office of the *Parliamentary Counsel* is responsible for drafting all government Bills, except Bills or provision of Bills relating exclusively to Scotland, which are handled by the Lord Advocate's Department (see p. 92). The office drafts all financial and other parliamentary motions and amendments moved by the government during the passage of legislation. It also advises departments on questions of parliamentary procedure and attends sittings (and committees) of both Houses of Parliament.

Parliamentary Counsel also draft subordinate legislation when specially instructed, and advise the Government on legal, parliamentary and constitutional questions falling within their special experience.

The *Statute Law Committee* comprises members of the judiciary and the legal profession in England, Wales and Scotland appointed by, and chaired by, the Lord Chancellor. It exercises a general supervision of the form of statute law and of statutory instruments, and is responsible for the publication of amended editions of the statutes, including the current official revised edition of the statutes in force.

Law Reform

The duty of keeping the law under review in order to ensure that it meets the needs of modern society lies mainly with a permanent *Law Commission*.

The *Law Commission* consists of five lawyers of high standing who are appointed by the Lord Chancellor with a full-time legal staff to assist them. They have the task of scrutinising the law and making recommendations for simplifying and modernising. Programmes of reform are submitted to the Lord Chancellor and are laid before Parliament.

Before a final report is submitted to the Lord Chancellor, a consultation paper is issued which sets out the present law on the topic, the difficulties which have arisen in connection with it (often comparing the law with that in other jurisdictions), and suggestions for possible ways of dealing with the difficulty. Comments are sought. Detailed recommendations for reform which are often largely influenced by the comments received, are published (usually with draft legislation appended). It is then open to the Government or an ordinary Member of Parliament to introduce proposals for reform as a parliamentary Bill.

The Commission also deals with the consolidation of the law, which involves bringing together in a single statute all the enactments on a particular subject, and with statute law revision, which involves removing obsolete laws from the statute book. The Law Commission was established in 1965. Since then it has published 207 reports including 26 annual reports and reports on legal topics ranging from divorce law to exemption clauses in contracts. Its annual report to the Lord Chancellor is laid before Parliament.

The Courts and the Executive

The courts normally use the same procedure in their dealings with public authorities as with private authorities. As judicial bodies, they cannot initiate proceedings. However, the rule of law asserts that every citizen is entitled to claim his or her rights in an ordinary law court. As a result the courts can and do intervene if asked to do so by a person seeking a legal remedy for an injury resulting from the act or omission of a public authority.

Public authorities, including central government departments (the Crown), are liable in ordinary civil action for torts (such as negligence or trespass), or breaches of contract. Their liability is broadly the same as that of private people. Actions for damages may be brought against public authorities or (in the case of the Central Government) the Attorney General if the complainant is not sure about the proper department to take action against. In some cases criminal proceedings can be brought against public authorities (for instance, for breaches of public health legislation).

Parties in civil proceedings can generally require the production of documents held by the Crown for the purposes of evidence. The courts accept the power of central government to withhold documents when genuine state secrets are involved, but disclosure may be ordered unless the public interest in secrecy outweighs the public interest in doing justice to the individual. This decision is made by the courts and not the Government.

Judicial Review

The wider powers of the courts to review governmental action start with the doctrine of *ultra vires*. Where public authorities and officials take on unauthorised functions, they are acting beyond their powers (*ultra vires*), and the courts can intervene to stop the illegal action. (Sometimes a decision which is within an authority's powers can be challenged on the ground that it was based on a misinterpretation of the law.) Judicial review is thus primarily a matter of statutory interpretation to make sure that the authority given by Parliament to a public body is not exceeded. The courts have also, however, applied judge-made rules alongside the rules set out in legislation. These have established a number of principles which are applied to all public authorities unless expressly excluded by legislation. They have, for example, frequently applied the 'rules of natural justice' as minimum fair standards of decision-making. The concept does not depend on the technicalities usually associated with courts of law. Instead it is based on two main rules: that the decision-maker must be free from bias—no one is to be a judge in their own cause—and that all parties to a dispute are to be given a fair hearing.

If an official body fails to carry out a duty, or exercises a power for an unauthorised purpose, or uses a power beyond the limits placed on it (although not for an illegal purpose), a wide range of remedies can be sought from the courts. These include prerogative orders, injunctions, declarations and statutory remedies.

Prerogative Orders

Prerogative orders are almost always issued from the Queen's Bench Division of the High Court (see p. 22). The decision on whether or not to make such an order rests with the court on the basis of the facts put before it by the parties to the dispute. The prerogative orders are *certiorari, prohibition* and *mandamus.*

Certiorari may be used to quash a decision (whether or not it affects the enforceable rights of an individual) that has already been made. It is available where an inferior court or administrative tribunal or authority has acted in excess or abuse of jurisdiction, or against the rules of natural justice, or where an error of law is apparent in the record of proceedings.

Prohibition may be used to prevent such bodies from acting or continuing to act in excess or abuse of jurisdiction, or contrary to the rules of natural justice. Both *certiorari* and prohibition are limited to the enforcement of judicial functions and are not concerned with legislative functions. Neither may be used to control the jurisdiction of purely domestic tribunals.

A court may refuse leave to apply for an order of *certiorari* if the application has not been made within six months of the proceedings which it is sought to challenge, unless the delay can be satisfactorily explained to the court. In addition, some administrative orders are statutorily excluded from judicial review and may be challenged only by means of the remedy provided for in the Act concerned.

Mandamus may be granted to compel the performance of a public duty owed to an applicant with a sufficient legal interest in its performance. It may be used for both legislative and judicial functions and is not subject to a time limit. As with other prerogative orders, it may be applied to public bodies, but not against the

Crown or Crown servants, at least where they are acting as advisers to the Crown.

Injunctions

An injunction is a court order restraining a person from doing something injurious to another's interests or commanding something to be done for the protection of another's interest. It is available in disputes between private individuals as well as between the subject and public authority. Injunctions cannot be taken out against the Crown, nor against Crown servants, but it is the remedy most often used against local government authorities and chartered and statutory corporations. An injunction may be interlocutory (given in the course of the legal action) or perpetual. It may be granted on a temporary basis during the action, even right at the beginning.

Declarations

A court may issue a declaration to declare the invalidity of administrative orders and delegated legislation, or to declare the applicant's rights, without necessarily referring to any decision of an administrative authority. Unlike a prerogative order a declaration can be granted in respect of domestic tribunals. Its availability does not depend on whether the applicant has an independent cause of action, but he or she must assert a real interest recognised in law. A declaration may be refused by the court on the grounds that the right or privilege for which it is sought has been conferred on the applicant by a statute which also provides a remedy for the protection of that right of privilege. It may also be refused, at the discretion of the court, on a number of other grounds.

A declaration is applied for in the same way and subject to the same procedure as an ordinary civil action. There is no time limit within which proceedings must be begun.

Statutory Remedies

Remedies against actions by public bodies are sometimes provided for by statute. The nature of the remedy depends on the particular statute. In some cases a statute provides for an application to review and then annul an authority's action. In other cases a statute provides for an appeal to a court regarding an authority's decision, usually on a point of law. An important difference between review and appeal is that in the case of review the court simply annuls a decision and the authority is then free to reconsider the matter; in the case of an appeal the court can usually substitute its own decision for that of the authority.

The Personnel of the Legal System

The operation of the law is based on the work of judicial officers, ranging from judges in the House of Lords and the superior courts to the stipendiary and lay magistrates. These, together with juries in certain cases, are responsible for deciding disputed cases. The legal system also depends on officers of the court who have general or specialised functions of an administrative, and sometimes of a judicial, nature in the courts to which they are attached. Barristers and solicitors represent the interests of parties to a dispute.

Lay Magistrates

Lay magistrates ('justices of the peace'—JPs) are appointed on behalf of the Crown by the Lord Chancellor who is advised by

committees in each county. In the Duchy of Lancaster, appointments are made by the Chancellor of the Duchy of Lancaster, a
Cabinet minister. Advisory committees are expected to ensure that
the candidates recommended to the Lord Chancellor are broadly
representative of the community which they will have to serve;
steps are also taken to ensure that no bench becomes unduly
weighted in favour of any one political party. There are a total of
28,000 magistrates. About 2,000 are appointed each year to replace
those who have died.

Magistrates do not have to have any legal qualifications
but are trained to give them sufficient knowledge of the law,
including the rules of evidence, and of the nature and purpose of
sentencing.

Lay magistrates are expected to attend court on at least 26
occasions every year (unless this is impossible because their bench
does not sit frequently enough); most attend more often. Although
they receive no salary for their work, they may be paid travelling
and subsistence allowances and a financial loss allowance—that
is to say a specified sum for actual loss of income or extra
expenses incurred in attendance at court. The statutory retirement
age is 70.

Judges
Appointments to the Circuit Bench and more senior judicial
appointments are made by the Crown, acting on the advice of min-
isters, reflecting the fact that the courts are the Queen's courts.
Recommendations for appointment to the highest positions—the
Lords of Appeal in Ordinary, the Lord Chief Justice, the Master of
the Rolls, the President of the Family Division, and the Lords
Justices who are the judges of the Court of Appeal—are made by

the Prime Minister. The Lord Chancellor recommends the High Court and circuit judges (see p. 17), the recorders (see p. 17) and the 76 metropolitan and stipendiary magistrates (see p. 16).

Political considerations play no part in the appointment of judges, except in the case of the Lord Chancellor (who, as well as being head of the judiciary, is a senior Cabinet Minister and the Speaker of the House of Lords).

Full-time judges are appointed from among other judges or practising lawyers. To qualify as a Lord Justice of Appeal or for appointment as Lord Chief Justice, Master of the Rolls or President of the Family Division, a candidate must either be a High Court judge or have had at least ten years rights of audience in relation to all proceedings in the High Court. A High Court judge must have had the same right of audience or have been a Circuit Judge for at least two years.

In certain circumstances—for instance, in cases of misconduct or proved incapacity—judges of the inferior courts may be removed from their position by the Lord Chancellor. However, in order to safeguard the independence of the judiciary from the executive, the position of superior judges is protected by Act of Parliament, and they may be removed by the Sovereign only if an address is presented by both Houses of Parliament.

Judges are immune from civil liability while acting in their judicial capacity. They have powers to punish litigants and members of the public for contempt of court.

The number of judges that may be appointed in the superior courts is laid down in Acts of Parliament. Judicial salaries are charged upon the Consolidated Fund so that, unlike other items of national expenditure, they do not have to be reviewed in Parliament each year. The salaries of circuit judges, recorders and stipendiary magistrates are set by the Lord Chancellor with the consent of the Minister for the Civil Service.

The statutory retirement age for judges of the superior courts is 75. Circuit judges are subject to retirement at 72, with a possible extension to 75. Retired judges receive a pension equal to half their salary if they have held office for 15 years, or a smaller pension for shorter service. In 1992 the Government introduced a Bill to reduce the maximum retirement age of all judges to 70, but with the possibility of extensions up to 75 where it is in the public interest.

Officers of the Supreme Court

Masters and Registrars
In 1992 there were 12 Masters of the Queen's Bench Division. In addition the Registrar of Criminal Appeals, who heads the Criminal Appeal Office (which is responsible for processing all appeals to the Criminal Division of the Court of Appeal), also holds office as Master of the Crown Office, and ranks as a Queen's Bench Master. The Master appointed to be Senior Master of the Queen's Bench Division also holds the office of Queen's Remembrancer.

The main duties of the Queen's Bench Masters include exercising the authority of a judge in chambers, issuing directions on points of practice, and assessing the amount of damages in cases where judgment is obtained in default because the claim is not contested. One of the Masters (who sit in rotation) acts as 'Practice Master', dealing with particular points of practice and procedure which may arise during the course of litigation. The Central Office, the principal office of the supreme court in which all proceedings other than Family Division cases are initiated, is under the general control of the Senior Master of the Queen's Bench Division.

The Masters of the Chancery Division (five in 1992) make interlocutory orders (see p. 24) under the direction of the judges to whom they are assigned. They are assisted by other officers whose duties are to take notes of the orders and judgments given and to draw up, settle and pass orders in court.

In the Family Division, duties similar to those carried out in other divisions by masters are discharged by district judges. The district judges deal with the ancillary or out-of-court work in divorce and other matrimonial matters, and with adoption, guardianship, wardship cases and work under the Children Act 1989.

There are also Bankruptcy Registrars and Registrars of the Companies Court, the Admiralty Registrar, the Master of the Court of Protection, and Taxing Masters (the latter are responsible for scrutinising and assessing solicitors' bills of costs).

The Masters and Registrars of the Supreme Court are appointed by the Lord Chancellor, with the Minister for the Civil Service's agreement on numbers and salaries.

The Official Solicitor
The Official Solicitor is concerned with the interests of minors and people suffering from mental disability who are involved in proceedings in the High Court and who would otherwise be unrepresented. In addition, he or she protects the interests of people committed to prison for contempt of court, acts as Receiver for people suffering from a mental disability, and can be appointed a judicial trustee in complex and disputed trusts. The Official Solicitor is sometimes called upon to help the court by instructing

counsel to give it independent advice in cases where important legal issues are involved, as well as by carrying out investigations or assisting in seeing that justice is done between parties.

Other Supreme Court Departments
Other Supreme Court offices include the *Court Funds Office* which is responsible for the control and management of funds in court, the receipt and payment of money into and out of court, and the investment of money on behalf of parties involved in litigation. They also include the *Court of Protection*, which deals with the management and protection of the property of those who are suffering from mental disorder and are therefore unable to manage their own affairs.

Unified Court Service

Administrative Staff
The courts in England and Wales are administered by the staff of a Unified Court Service in the Lord Chancellor's Office. The Court Service is administered from a headquarters in London and from offices in the six circuits into which, for this purpose, England and Wales are divided. Each circuit is under the control of a senior official called the Circuit Administrator. The circuits are themselves divided into areas, each of which is the responsibility of a Courts Administrator. The responsibilities of these officials include the deployment of judges and recorders in accordance with the flow of work, and the handling of all matters concerning the administrative staff of the courts. Each Circuit Administrator works closely with the 'presiding judges' of his or her circuit. These are the judges of the High Court, two of whom are allocated to each circuit (three to

the south-eastern circuit) to supervise and advise on the judicial aspects of the work.

There are also a number of advisory committees appointed by the Lord Chancellor in each circuit and consisting of lawyers, magistrates, police officers and representatives of the probation service, the local authorities and the press. Their meetings are normally chaired by the circuit administrator, who may seek their advice on particular matters.

The Legal Profession

The legal profession is divided into two branches: barristers (known collectively as the 'Bar' and collectively and individually as counsel) and solicitors.

Barristers

Barristers give expert legal opinions to solicitors and their clients (some spend most of their time on this type of work) and conduct cases in court. With certain exceptions such as international work and instructions from members of approved professional bodies, barristers can act only on the instructions of a solicitor, to whom a lay client must go in the first instance. Traditionally barristers have had an exclusive right of audience in all but the lowest civil and criminal courts. These restrictions are being removed (see p. 58).

There are some 6,900 barristers practising in England and Wales; about 1,270 are women and about 350 are members of the ethnic minorities. Three-quarters of barristers practise in London. Of all practising barristers, about one in ten is a 'Queen's Counsel' (QC), an appointment granted to certain senior barristers by the Queen on the recommendation of the Lord Chancellor. A Queen's Counsel is known as a 'silk' because of his or her entitlement to a silk gown instead of a stuff (or woollen) one. Barristers who are not Queen's Counsel are known as 'juniors', whatever their age.

Every barrister—and every student wishing to become a barrister—must be a member of one of the four *Inns of Court*— Lincoln's Inn, Inner Temple, Middle Temple and Gray's Inn. The Inn remains the barrister's professional home throughout his or her career. Each Inn is governed by Masters of the Bench ('Benchers') selected from its senior members. Every practising barrister normally occupies 'chambers' with perhaps 15 colleagues, sharing the services of a clerk and junior staff.

Students of the Inns of Court normally have a degree in law from a university or polytechnic. Those with degrees in other subjects who intend to become barristers may become student members of an Inn. Those who wish to become barristers practising in the courts of England and Wales and the European Community must take the vocational course at the Inns of Court School of Law. Non-law graduates must first complete the one year Common Professional Examination course which provides a grounding in academic law. Students who do not intend to practice at the independent Bar—for instance, those intending to practice overseas— may take the Bar Finals course at one of a number of independent colleges. Students must keep terms of dining in the hall of the appropriate Inn a given number of times. Afterwards students are eligible to be 'called to the Bar', but may not practise as advocates in independent practice until they have completed a year's 'pupillage' with an established barrister.

The governing body of the profession is the General Council of the Bar which consists of elected members. Its functions include responsibility for maintaining standards and the independence of the Bar, investigating complaints and disciplinary matters, promoting and preserving the services of the Bar and representing the Bar in its relations with others and in matters affecting the administration of justice. It is also responsible for the policy of the Council of Legal Education.

Solicitors

Solicitors undertake all ordinary legal business for clients (with whom they are in direct contact), including the preliminary conduct of litigation and numerous non-litigious matters such as the conveyancing of land and houses, the drawing up of wills, and the provision of legal advice on matters ranging from the domestic to those affecting public affairs. Solicitors undertake legal business for individual and corporate clients, while barristers advise on legal problems submitted through solicitors and present cases in the higher courts. (Restrictions on the services provided by barristers and solicitors are being removed—see p. 58.) Both professions can present cases in the lower courts. Although people are free to conduct their own cases, most people prefer to be legally represented in the more serious cases.

People who wish to become solicitors must be considered suitable by the appropriate committee of *The Law Society* (a chartered corporation which serves as the solicitors' professional body). After acceptance they must enter into training contracts with a practising solicitor of not less than five years' standing. As well as training during the term of these contracts prospective solicitors must pass professional examinations prescribed by the Law Society.

After admission, a solicitor may be made a partner in, or work as a salaried assistant in, an established firm but may not practise as a sole principal. He or she may also join large organisations which employ full-time legally qualified staff, including government

A cartoon from 1873 showing Sir James Bacon, a judge.

An impression of the interior of a court at the Old Bailey during the nineteenth century.

An illustration, dating from 1907, showing a murderer being sentenced to death.

The judges' procession to the House of Lords.

The present Lord Chancellor, the
Rt Hon The Lord Mackay of Clashfern.

Interior of a sheriff's court in Glasgow.

A judge. A review of court dress is in
progress.

Administering the oath to a police witness
in a magistrate's court.

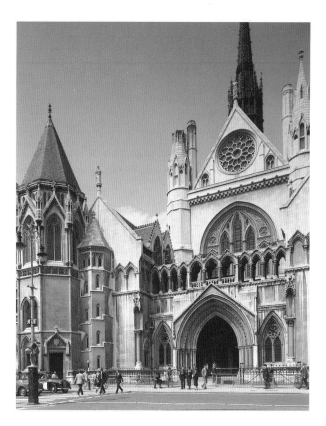

The Royal Courts of Justice (civil law courts) in the Strand, London.

A law centre in North Kensington, London.

departments. Solicitors may also work for local government; quali-fication as a solicitor is often required for appointments to the posi-tion of town clerk or chief executive. Out of a total of some 70,000 solicitors there are some 57,000 practising in England and Wales, of whom over 14,000 are women and some 1,000 members of ethnic minorities.

Solicitors are officers of the court, and in theory are amenable to the direct discipline of the judges (unlike barristers who have always enjoyed a completely detached position). In practice com-plaints are received and investigated by the Solicitors' Complaints Bureau which may refer matters to the Solicitors' Disciplinary Tribunal which is appointed by the Master of the Rolls. The Disciplinary Tribunal investigates charges of misconduct and may impose penalties. There is an appeal against its decisions to a Divisional Court of the Queen's Bench Division and, with leave of the court, to the Civil Division of the Court of Appeal and there-after to the House of Lords.

Legal Services Ombudsman

The system of complaints against legal practitioners has been strengthened by the creation, under the Courts and Legal Services Act, of a Legal Services Ombudsman able to investigate how the professional bodies handle these complaints. The Ombudsman has the power to recommend the payment of compensation.

Courts and Legal Services Act 1990

The Courts and Legal Services Act 1990 confirmed the existing advocacy and litigation rights of barristers and solicitors. It also opened the way for other professional bodies to apply these rights for their members, either as completely new rights or by extending existing rights. The Law Society has already applied to extend solicitors' rights of audience to the higher courts. The Act also contains provisions which would allow building societies, banks and other financial organisations to offer conveyancing services under a scheme providing new safeguards to clients. It has been decided not to implement these at present. People will also be able to negotiate a form of 'no win, no fee' agreement with their legal advisers in certain types of case. The implementation of the new legislation is currently under discussion.

Legal Aid

A person in need of legal advice or legal representation in court may qualify for help with the costs out of public funds under the various legal aid schemes. This may amount to the full costs or part of the costs, according to the person's own financial means.

Legal Advice and Assistance (Green Form) Scheme

People whose income and savings are within certain limits—which vary according to the types of legal help required—are entitled to help from a solicitor on legal matters (with the exception of conveyancing and, in some cases, making a will). Such help may include advice on the relevant law, writing letters on the client's behalf, and taking the opinion of a barrister. A variant of the scheme also covers representation in civil proceedings in the magistrates' courts and hearings of the Mental Health Review Tribunal. The basic Green Form scheme allows for solicitors to do up to three hours' worth of work for matrimonial cases where a petition is drafted and two hours' worth for other work. These limits may be extended with the approval of the Legal Aid Board.

Legal Aid in Civil Proceedings

Legal aid, which covers representation before the court, is available for most civil proceedings to those who satisfy the financial eligibility conditions. Applicants for legal aid must show not only that they have reasonable grounds for taking or defending proceedings—or being party to proceedings—but also that it is reasonable that they should receive legal aid. If legal aid is granted, it covers the costs incurred by the applicant's solicitors, and, where appropriate, counsel. Payments to solicitors are made through the Legal Aid Fund administered by the Legal Aid Board.

In certain limited circumstances the successful unassisted opponent of a legally aided party may recover his or her costs in the case from the Legal Aid Fund. Where the assisted person recovers or preserves money or property in the proceedings, the Legal Aid Fund will usually have a first charge on that money or property to recover money spent on the assisted person's behalf.

Legal Aid in Criminal Proceedings

In criminal proceedings the court may make a legal aid order if it appears to be in the interests of justice and if a defendant is considered to need assistance in meeting his or her costs. A certificate must be granted (subject to means) when a person is committed for trial on a murder charge or where the prosecutor appeals or applies for leave to appeal from the Court of Appeal to the House of Lords. No person who is unrepresented can be given a custodial sentence for the first time unless given the opportunity to be represented by a lawyer and, if appropriate, apply for legal aid.

The Legal Aid Board in England and Wales makes arrangements for duty solicitors to be present at magistrates' courts to provide initial advice and representation to unrepresented defendants.

Solicitors are available, on a 24-hour basis, to give advice and assistance to suspects at police stations. The services both of a solicitor at a police station and the duty solicitor at a court are free and are not means tested.

Law Centres

In a number of urban areas law centres provide free legal advice and representation. Financed from various sources, often including local government authorities, they usually employ full-time salaried lawyers and many have community workers. Much of their time is devoted to housing, employment, social security and immigration problems.

Free advice is also available in Citizens Advice Bureaux, consumer and housing advice centres, and in specialist advice centres run by various voluntary organisations.

The Legal System of Scotland

Origins of Scots Law

Scots law belongs to a small group of 'mixed' legal systems which have legal principles, rules and concepts modelled on both Roman and English law. The main sources of Scots law are judge-made law, certain legal treatises having 'institutional' authority, legislation, and European Community law. The first two sources are sometimes referred to as the common law of Scotland. Legislation, as in the rest of Britain, consists of statutes (Acts of Parliament) or subordinate legislation authorised by Parliament. Subordinate legislation falls into two main groups. The first consists of Orders-in-Council (made by the Queen in Council) and orders, rules and regulations made by a Minister of the Crown. These almost invariably take the form of 'statutory instruments' which are published and are subject to parliamentary scrutiny and control. They normally apply throughout Scotland. Many procedural rules of the Scottish courts are also contained in statutory instruments: 'acts of sederunt' made by the Court of Session to regulate procedure in that Court or the sheriff court in civil proceedings, and 'acts of adjournal' made by the High Court of Justiciary for regulating criminal procedure in that Court or the summary criminal courts. The second main type of subordinate legislation consists of by-laws which have local effect and are made by local authorities or other public authorities exercising powers delegated by Parliament.

In contrast to some European countries Scots law is not codified.

Common Law

Scoto-Norman Law
In the eleventh and twelfth centuries Scotland became a feudal
kingdom on the European pattern as a result of the royal policy of
granting land to Anglo-Normans, together with Celtic and other
indigenous chiefs, in return for military and other feudal services.
These feudal land grants carried the right to hold courts, and justice was mainly dispensed in local feudal courts. The sheriff—the
King's local representative (whose office became hereditary)—held
a court manned by local landowners. The barony courts consisted
of the lord and his vassals (those holding land on condition that
they offered homage and allegiance). They heard cases between
vassal and vassal or between the lord and his vassals, involving feudal obligations and other disputes. The burghs (or towns) had their
own courts.

In medieval theory the King was the source of all secular justice, and his officials supervised the civil and criminal work of local
courts and heard cases reserved by law to the King. The church
courts, applying the general canon law of western Christendom,
possessed exclusive jurisdiction over family relations, succession to
moveable property, and some other matters.

Much of the early law concerned procedure. By the end of the
thirteenth century, archaic forms of proof, such as trial by battle or
by ordeal, had been rejected in favour of more modern methods,
including the civil jury. The English system of initiating legal proceedings with a writ was adopted. In Scotland the writ was called a
'brieve' and was issued by the royal chancery; it usually instructed
the local courts to convene a jury to hold an inquiry into the case.
However the enormous range of writs found in England was not

copied; instead, the system was simplified to make it appropriate to a small and relatively poor country.

Although few judicial records of the period have survived, the diverse origins of Scots law in this period are illustrated by the most important single source of medieval law, *Regiam Majestatem*, a commentary on judicial procedures dating from the thirteenth or early fourteenth century. About two-thirds of its contents derive from an older English treatise, some rules from Celtic law and the remaining rules from Roman and canon law.

The Development of a National System of Law

After the wars of independence against the English, culminating in the Scottish victory at the Battle of Bannockburn (1314), Scotland's external ties were mainly with France and the Low Countries rather than with England. The existing system of brieves and jury inquest continued to be developed (new types of brieve were created until the fifteenth century), but direct borrowing from England ceased. Instead, until the universities which were established in Scotland in the fifteenth century began to give an adequate training in law, many Scottish lawyers studied overseas. The universities at which they studied, in France and Flanders and, after the Reformation, The Netherlands, all taught Roman Law.

In the unstable conditions of the late Middle Ages, there was a constant demand for royal justice. In response, a committee of Parliament (called the Lords Auditors of Causes and Complaints) and a committee of the King's Privy Council (called the Lords of Council and Session) supplemented the jurisdiction of the royal justiciars and eventually replaced it in civil cases.

This period of experimentation ended in 1532 when the Lords of Council and Session were reorganised on a permanent basis as a

College of Justice with a wide (though not universal) civil jurisdiction. The judges of 'the Session' became Senators of the College of Justice and sat as a collegiate court of 15 judges. At first the president and half the judges were drawn from the clergy, but in time the number of churchmen diminished; after 1668 the judges were always laymen.

In the course of the sixteenth century the Faculty of Advocates and the Society of Writers to the Signet evolved, and their members became members of the College of Justice with the exclusive privilege of acting as pleaders (advocates) and solicitors respectively. The evolution of a professional judiciary and bar was associated with the creation of a modern system of procedure, closely modelled on the Romano-canonical system. This system had been developed by the Church courts and strongly influenced secular procedure throughout Western Europe, except in the English common law courts. These influences are evident in the first vernacular treatises on Scottish judicial procedure, Sir John Skene's *Short Form of Proces* (1609) and Habakkuk Bisset's *Rolment of Courtis* (1622). These show that Scots law had taken a quite different course from English law in at least three ways:

1. In England, from the twelfth century to the 1870s, specific forms of action in the common law courts were initiated by a closed category of writs, each of which was appropriate to a closely defined category of legal claims. Each had its own technical name and procedural peculiarities. Hence it is said that the establishment of a right depended on the existence of a remedy (see p. 6). By contrast, in Scotland, judicial procedure was general in character. Proceedings in the Court of Session were initiated, not by brieves, but by a single form of summons which could be adapted to an infinite variety of different claims.

Remedies depended on rights and there were few procedural barriers to litigation provided the court had jurisdiction over the litigants or the subject matter in dispute.

2. Scots law was a unitary system. Although it recognised a distinction between strict law on the one hand and judges exercising discretionary powers equitably to mitigate the strict rigours of the law on the other, it did not follow English law in making equity into a separate system of law supplementing the common law with its own rules, procedure and courts.

3. In the Scottish central courts, cases were tried by judges; the brieve and jury system were restricted to local courts, whereas the English common law courts used juries to decide on issues of fact in all forms of civil action.

Despite advances in judicial procedure, the substantive law was for a long time too uncertain and ill-defined. To fill the many gaps left by feudal, customary and statute law, the judges and practitioners in the Court of Session turned to Roman law. In response to the need for the consistent application and development of the law, reports of the Court of Session's decisions were circulated among the few court practitioners in unofficial manuscript collections. However, such reports gave only a summary of decisions and did not provide a framework within which the law could develop.

A major advance in the creation of the system of civil law was made in 1681, when Lord Stair, Lord President of the Court of Session, published the *Institutions of the Law of Scotland*. This set out the whole of Scots law as a rational, comprehensive, and practical system of rules based on commonsense principles. As far as possible, Stair drew his law from Scottish decisions and statutes; otherwise he was guided by Roman or canon law, or Romano-Germanic systems. Later 'institutional' restatements incorporated such new law as had either been developed by judicial decisions or enacted in statutes.

In civil law Erskine's *Institute* (1773) and Bell's *Commentaries* (1800) were particularly important. Baron Hume's *Commentaries* on criminal law set out systematically Scottish criminal law as it had been developed by the High Court of Justiciary which had been founded in 1672.

Following the Union of the Parliaments of Scotland and England and the formation of the United Kingdom of Great Britain in 1707,[11] the House of Lords became the supreme court of appeal in civil but not criminal proceedings.

The Modern Law

At about the end of the eighteenth century, English law replaced Roman law as the main external source of Scots law. This reflected the fact that the practice of studying law on the Continent declined in the eighteenth century, and was finally brought to an end by the Napoleonic Wars. As Scotland moved towards English legal methods, the doctrine of 'judicial precedent' (see p. 5) came to be more strictly applied. Its acceptance was further assisted by the introduction of procedures whereby, in written pleadings and judgments, questions of fact were separated clearly from questions of law so that the precise legal principle or rule applied by the court could be more clearly discerned. In addition, from about the 1820s onwards, full reports of judicial decisions were published regularly. Other influences tending to bring Scots and English law together included decisions given in civil cases in the House of Lords, the majority of whose judges have always been English lawyers

[11]For further details, see *Scotland* (Aspects of Britain: HMSO, forthcoming).

untrained in Scots law. The common industrial and commercial experience of Britain also raised problems unknown to Roman law to which English law had found solutions.

Today Roman law and continental legal systems are very rarely referred to in the courts as living sources of Scots law. In the many areas of Scots law which are uninfluenced by English law, the courts develop the law having regard only to existing Scottish sources. A decision of the House of Lords in an appeal from the English courts is not binding on the Scottish courts, but in practice a decision of the House in a civil appeal is usually regarded as of highly persuasive authority if the case concerns principles which apply in both legal systems. Decisions of other English and Scottish courts do not bind each other, although English decisions have persuasive authority in Scotland (and *vice versa*). This is especially true with cases involving United Kingdom statutes where uniformity is desirable (for example, laws dealing with taxation).

Despite English influence, civil law in Scotland rests more on generalised rights than in England and the remedy depends on the right rather than, as in the English tradition, the right on the remedy. In addition Scots law retains a tendency to argue from principles to cases, rather than to draw its abstract principles from particular cases. There are also many differences between the contents of the principles and rules in civil law and procedure and, even more so, in criminal law and procedure.

The present structure of the judicial system dates largely from the period since the Union of 1707. As a result of statutory reforms in the early nineteenth century, the Court of Session absorbed the Commissary, Admiralty and Exchequer Courts and also the new Jury Court which had been formed in 1815 to introduce trial by jury on the English model in civil jurisdiction. Following the

Rebellion of 1745 the heritable jurisdictions were abolished. In due course the sheriff courts, presided over by full-time, legally qualified judges, became the pre-eminent local courts with a very wide civil and criminal jurisdiction.

Legislation

As an independent state before 1707, Scotland possessed a Parliament of its own which had developed in the late Middle Ages and become the most important central law-making institution. Certain Acts of the Scottish Parliament are still in force, although many are being repealed as the law is gradually modernised. In 1707, the United Kingdom of Great Britain was created by the Acts of Union; in law the Scottish and English Parliaments ceased to exist, and the Parliament of the United Kingdom, having English and Scottish members and peers, was constituted as a new legal institution. The Acts include certain safeguards for, among other things, Scots law and the Scottish courts. Article XVIII provides that, while:

> 'the laws which concern public and civil government may be made the same throughout the whole United Kingdom ... no alteration be made in the laws which concern private right, except for the evident utility of the subjects within Scotland.'

No procedure is laid down for determining how 'evident utility' should be ascertained, and the concept of 'private right' was not defined. Article XIX stipulates that the Court of Session and High Court of Justiciary are to continue and are not to be subject to the jurisdiction of the English courts.

Under the doctrine of parliamentary sovereignty, Acts of Parliament are absolutely binding on all courts and take precedence over other sources of law such as rights conferred by the common law. According to the doctrine any Act of the British Parliament can repeal or amend former statutes whether of the British Parliament, or of the Scottish or English Parliaments: the courts cannot challenge Parliament's power of repeal or amendment. This view is accepted in Scotland but there are differences over whether the safeguards for Scottish courts and Scots law impose legal limitations upon parliamentary sovereignty.

In England there is a consensus that the constitutional safeguards in Articles XVIII and XIX of the Acts of Union can be repealed or amended in the same way as any other Act of Parliament. In Scotland this view has been challenged on the grounds that it undervalues the fundamental character of the Acts of Union. For example, in evidence to the Royal Commission on the Constitution published in 1973, the Faculty of Advocates in Scotland pointed out that:

'In the Scottish mind, emphasis is placed on the origin of the United Kingdom Parliament in a freely negotiated Union between two equals, the sovereign legislatures of Scotland and England. Notwithstanding the numerical preponderance of English members in the Parliament of Great Britain, it was not created by the admission to the English Parliament of Scottish Members, but by the establishment of a new legislature for Great Britain as a whole.'

There has been no case in which the judges have held a particular statute to be null as infringing the Acts of Union and the question has rarely been the subject of litigation, in part because governments sponsoring legislation and Parliament have usually respected the spirit of the terms of Union. Statutes have infringed the fundamental terms only where a consensus of Scottish opinion has approved the infringement—as in the case of nineteenth century legislation affecting the Scottish universities and courts. There have been two cases, decided in 1953 and 1975, in which Scottish judges expressly 'reserved their opinion' about the legal validity of any Act of Parliament which purported to abolish the Court of Session or to substitute English law for the whole body of Scots private law.

The special position of Scotland and its legal system is recognised within Parliament by the establishment of a Scottish Grand Committee and Scottish Standing Committees of the House of Commons for the more important stages of consideration of Bills applying only to Scotland (or—and perhaps more frequently—of Bills which, since they relate mainly to Scotland, the House of Commons has ordered to be proceeded with *as if* applying only to Scotland).[12]

Branches of Scots Law

The two most important branches of Scots law are civil law and criminal law. While the application of specific rules is generally fixed by law, the boundaries of the larger categories of Scots law, though well enough understood, are not laid down authoritatively (for example, in codes). Instead the boundaries tend to be drawn by the authors of legal text-books and by university teachers, having regard to tradition, practical convenience, ease of exposition and gradual changes in legal thought. Broadly speaking, Parliament and the courts make the specific principles and rules while the writers on law classify and organise these principles and rules in larger categories. There are exceptions to this generalisation, including Great Britain or United Kingdom statutes (see p. 67). There have

[12]For further details, see *Parliament* (Aspects of Britain: HMSO, 1991).

also been statutes codifying large parts of the Scots law of civil and criminal procedure and bankruptcy.

Criminal Law

As in England and Wales the general distinction between criminal and civil law is that criminal law deals with acts for which the state may prosecute in the criminal courts while civil law concerns acts dealt with by the civil courts. (Private prosecutions in the criminal courts are possible, although infrequent.) Crimes are therefore defined by statute or the common law as clearly as possible so that people may be aware of the restrictions on their freedom of action. The prosecution must prove that the accused intended to commit the act (or default) constituting the offence with which he or she is charged, but there are a few exceptions to this general rule.

The more serious crimes are tried by judge and jury on *indictment*. Less serious crimes are tried on *summary complaint* by the judge of an inferior court sitting without a jury.

The law of criminal evidence and procedure governs the proof of the facts alleged in criminal proceedings and the procedures between the arrest of the accused and the disposal of the case by the court at the trial or on appeal.

Civil Law: Private Law

Civil law comprises private law, concerning the rights and obligations of individuals among themselves, and public law which deals with the functions of the state (other than its duty of criminal prosecution) and with public authorities.

The more important branches of private law include:

—*family law*, which, for example, regulates marriage, divorce, and the guardianship and custody of children;

—the *law of contract*, which concerns sale of goods, hire-purchase, employment, loans, insurance and partnership;

—*the law of delict*, which deals mainly with civil wrongs for which the wrongdoer must pay compensation, such as defamation, damage to property or personal injury caused by negligence;

—*the law of property*, whether corporeal or incorporeal, which concerns rights over property; and

—*mercantile law*—e.g. contract, companies, and bankruptcy.

International private law regulates the jurisdiction of the Scottish courts in cases where foreigners or foreign property are involved. It determines whether Scots law or foreign law (in the sense of a legal system distinct from Scots law, including English law and Northern Irish law) is applicable to a legal question; it also provides for the recognition and enforcement in Scotland of foreign judgments.

Other Branches of Civil Law

Public law includes *constitutional* and *administrative law*. These branches of the law deal with the creation, regulation and control by law of political and administrative power within the state, and concern the relations, one to another, of Parliament, the courts, central and local government, public authorities and the individual citizen. The *laws of civil evidence and procedure* govern respectively the proof of facts in civil proceedings and the various steps of procedure to be followed in civil litigation.

Service Law

Service law, concerning the armed forces, is contained in statutes based on English law (see p. 13).

Courts of Law

Civil Courts

The civil courts are the Court of Session, the supreme central court (subject only to the House of Lords in London), and the sheriff court, the principal local court.

The Court of Session

The Court of Session sits in the Parliament House in Edinburgh. Its governing principle is that cases originating in the Court are both prepared for decision, and are decided, by judges sitting alone. Their decisions are subject to review by a number of judges. The total number of judges in post is 25, of whom 16, called Lords Ordinary, are mainly concerned with preparing and deciding cases in the first instance. This branch of the Court is called the Outer House. The nine other judges are divided into two Divisions of four judges each; the ninth judge is assigned to the Scottish Law Commission (see p. 93). The quorum is three: the two Divisions form the Inner House. Normally the First Division is presided over by the Lord President of the Court of Session and the Second Division by the Lord Justice-Clerk. The main business of each Division is to review the decisions of the Lords Ordinary or inferior courts which are the subject of appeals to it.

The Court of Session is still a collegiate court, in spite of its subdivisions and hierarchical structure. The collegiate character is reflected in the fact that appeals from the Outer to the Inner House are called 'reclaiming motions'. A Lord Ordinary may report a case to the Inner House for guidance and one Division of the Inner House may consult the other. In cases of difficulty or importance, a fuller court, usually of seven judges, may be convened. Indeed, the whole court may sit together to decide a case but this practice is now rarely adopted.

The Inner House Divisions and Lords Ordinary are not required by law to specialise in specific categories of business. The officials of the General and Petition Departments of the Court of Session allocate cases to particular Lords Ordinary and the Divisions of the Inner House. It is, however, possible for parties, by agreement, to refer for summary trial some disputes to a judge chosen by them. A judge may also act as arbiter.

The Court of Session may hear cases arising in any part of Scotland. It alone can deal with cases where the court exercises private jurisdiction such as actions for divorce. The Court also has exclusive jurisdiction in actions to set aside or annul judicial decrees, and in petitions to vary private or public trusts or to wind up companies whose paid up capital exceeds £120,000.

A wide range of actions may be brought either in the Court of Session or sheriff court: examples include actions for damages and actions for recovery of debt (exceeding £1,500 in value); actions relating to the interpretation and implementation of contracts and other writings; certain actions concerning family matters (for example, custody of children); and certain actions relating to heritable right or title. Much of the litigation in the Court of Session concerns damages for personal injuries.

The Court has an equitable power, known as its 'noble office' (*nobile officium*), to provide a remedy where none is available under existing legislation or common law, and to mitigate the rigours of the law where these would lead to injustice—for example, to allow a mistake in procedure to be rectified. The Court has, however, set limits to this power, so that it is now exercised on comparatively rare occasions and then only where there is a precedent or analogy. In this way, powers to grant certain remedies (for example, the making of schemes for public trusts and the grant of directions to trustees), have come to be governed by precedents like other areas of the common law of Scotland.

The Sheriff Court

The sheriff court has jurisdiction over most civil litigation. Although there is no upper monetary limit, it considers all cases with a value not exceeding £1,500. Appeals may be made to the sheriff principal and/or to the Court of Session in ordinary actions. In summary causes (generally cases where the value of the claim is between £750 and £1,500) the case may be appealed to the sheriff principal on a point of law and then to the Court of Session only if the sheriff principal certifies the case as suitable for such an appeal. In small claims cases (where the value of the claim does not exceed £750) there may be an appeal to the sheriff principal only on a point of law.

Courts of Special Jurisdiction

The Court of Session sits as the *Court of Exchequer* when it hears 'exchequer cases', which consist mainly of appeals from the Special Commissioners of Income Tax. An appeal lies to the House of Lords.

There are three courts exercising final appellate jurisdiction and staffed by judges of the Court of Session. The *Registration of Voters Appeal Court* hears appeals from the sheriff concerning registration of parliamentary electors. The *Election Petition Court* hears petitions initiated in the courts to set aside the election of Members of Parliament—for example, on the grounds of corruption or illegality. The *Lands Valuation Appeal Court* hears appeals from the determination of local valuation appeal committees as to the rateable value of land and houses for local fiscal purposes. These courts are administered by officials of the Court of Session.

The *Restrictive Practices Court*, a British court (see p. 31), includes a judge of the Court of Session among its five judges. The *Scottish Land Court*, which deals exclusively with matters concerning agriculture, mainly in the 'crofting counties', consists of a judge (who is equal in rank to the judges of the Court of Session) and four laypeople who are specialists in agriculture. Although the Court is based in Edinburgh, it can sit, as required, in various rural centres throughout Scotland.

The *courts of the Church of Scotland*, the established church, are technically civil courts of the realm but only have jurisdiction over the members of the Church. The courts are the same bodies as the main organs of the church and form a four-tier hierarchy— Kirk Sessions; Presbyteries; Synods; and, at the summit of the hierarchy, the General Assembly of the Church of Scotland.

The *Court of the Lord Lyon King of Arms* has an historic jurisdiction in disputes concerning the right to bear coats of arms.

Administrative Tribunals

As in England and Wales, administrative tribunals consist of persons or bodies exercising judicial or quasi-judicial functions but which are not technically courts of law. Tribunals in Scotland operate on a similar basis to those in England and Wales (see p. 29).

Children's Hearings and Children's Panels

All children under 16 years who may be in need of compulsory measures of care are referred, by a local authority official called 'the reporter', to a tribunal of three ordinary citizens, known as a children's hearing. These are drawn from the children's panel for the local authority area. The sheriff intervenes only if the alleged facts are disputed.

Criminal Courts

There are three criminal courts in Scotland: the High Court of Justiciary, the sheriff court and the district court. The High Court deals with serious crimes, the sheriff courts (and district courts where presided over by stipendiary magistrates) with the less serious crimes and the lay district courts with minor offences.

Scotland has two types of criminal procedure, known as *solemn procedure* and *summary procedure*.

In solemn procedure, the trial of the accused takes place before a judge sitting with a jury of 15 laypeople, and the offence with which the accused is charged is set out in a document called an indictment. The judge decides questions of law; the jury decides questions of fact and may reach a decision by a simple majority.

In summary procedure, the judge sits without a jury and decides questions of both fact and law. The offence with which the individual is charged is set out in a writ called a summary complaint.

The High Court of Justiciary

The High Court of Justiciary is Scotland's supreme criminal court. There is no appeal from it to the House of Lords. The judges of the High Court are the same persons as the judges of the Court of

Session. However, as judges of the High Court, they are called Lord Commissioners of Justiciary and wear different robes. The head of the court is the Lord Justice-General (who in the Court of Session is the Lord President) and the judge next in seniority is the Lord Justice-Clerk. Unlike the Court of Session, the High Court sits in a number of towns. Appeals, however, are always heard in Edinburgh.

The High Court's jurisdiction extends throughout Scotland, and covers all categories of crime not specifically reserved to another court. It shares jurisdiction with the sheriff court over most crimes, but it has an exclusive jurisdiction over treason, murder, rape, obstruction of officers of court (called 'deforcement of messengers'), and breach of duty by magistrates.

The High Court is both a trial court and an appeal court. When it sits as a trial court, procedure is always solemn and usually only one of the judges takes the case. When it sits as the Court of Appeal, it consists of at least three judges, sitting without a jury.

The Court may authorise a retrial if it sets aside a conviction. The Lord Advocate may seek the opinion of the High Court on a point of law arising from a case where a person has been acquitted. The acquittal is not affected.

The Sheriff Court

The sheriff court has both solemn and summary jurisdiction. Most prosecutions are brought as summary complaints before one of the sheriffs. In contrast to civil proceedings, the sheriff principal does not hear appeals and may act only as a trial judge. The sentencing powers of the sheriff court are more limited than those of the High Court. Except where statute provides otherwise, the sheriff may impose an unlimited fine on conviction on indictment, while the maximum periods of imprisonment which can be imposed are three years on indictment and three or, in certain circumstances, six months in summary cases, depending on the statute contravened or the accused person's previous records. Where a case tried on indictment merits more severe penalties, the sheriff can remit it to the High Court for sentence.

The District Court
Since 1975 there have been district courts in each of the 56 district and islands areas (with the exception of the Orkney and Shetland area where there would have been insufficient business for the court). The district courts, presided over by lay justices, deal summarily with less serious statutory and common law offences. The maximum period of imprisonment that can be imposed is generally 60 days. When the court is presided over by a full-time legally qualified stipendiary magistrate it has the same summary criminal jurisdiction and powers as a sheriff has in summary procedure.

Procedure

Criminal Cases
The Scottish system of criminal justice and procedure is very different from that in England and Wales.

Public Prosecutions
The Lord Advocate, the principal Law Officer of the Crown in Scotland, is responsible for prosecutions in the High Court, the sheriff courts and the district courts. He or she is a Minister of the Crown and is generally responsible to Parliament for the operation of those government departments under his or her charge (the

Lord Advocate's Department, the Crown Office, and the Scottish Courts Administration). By constitutional convention the Lord Advocate is not required to give reasons for having exercised discretion as prosecutor in a particular way. However, he or she may answer questions in Parliament on the conduct of these responsibilities.

The Lord Advocate is assisted by the Solicitor General (the other Law Officer), but in turn they delegate the bulk of their work to the Advocates-Depute of whom there are currently 12. The two Law Officers and the Advocates-Depute are practising advocates and are known as 'Crown counsel'. The Advocates-Depute devote about half their time to Crown work and during the period of their appointment do not engage in any criminal defence work. Crown counsel work along with a small staff of officials (all of whom are full-time civil servants) headed by the Crown Agent. The whole central organisation is known as the Crown Office. As the headquarters of the administration of criminal prosecution, the Crown Office is concerned with the preparation of prosecutions in the High Court and the direction and control of the Procurator Fiscal Service.

Procurators-Fiscal

The procurators fiscal are the public prosecutors in the sheriff and district courts. They are full-time civil servants. They must either be advocates or solicitors, but are usually solicitors. The police report the details of a crime to the procurators fiscal, who have an absolute discretion whether or not to prosecute, subject to the general direction and control of the Crown Council. In contrast to the situation in England, private prosecutions are extremely rare. The police cannot initiate criminal proceedings. A few public authorities have statutory power to bring prosecutions for specific offences, but in practice these authorities now refer such offences to the procurators fiscal. Although prosecutions under statutory power by education authority nominees against parents for allowing truancy, or prosecutions by individuals for poaching still occur, such cases are nowadays exceptional.

The procurator fiscal investigates sudden or suspicious deaths, deaths occurring during the course of employment, and deaths in prison or police custody. They also investigate other suspicious occurrences such as fire and explosions and normally represent the Crown in fatal accident and sudden death inquiries.

The function of investigating crime is carried out by the police on behalf of the procurator fiscal, although the fiscal may take personal charge of investigations of serious or complex crimes. If the procurator fiscal decides provisionally that the offence is important enough to warrant prosecution on indictment, he or she brings the charge by way of petition. The accused then goes before the sheriff for judicial examination in private with only the sheriff clerk, procurator fiscal, solicitor for the accused, and police escorts in attendance.

At the judicial examination, the fiscal can move for committal of the accused for further examination or trial and the sheriff may consider an application for bail. The accused may apply for bail at this stage as well as later stages and may appeal to the High Court against refusal of bail. There are strict rules to ensure that the accused person does not spend an unduly long period in custody awaiting trial. The maximum period is normally 110 days.

Trial

In *solemn procedure* a jury of 15 is empanelled and sworn unless the accused pleads 'guilty'. The indictment is read. The prosecutors are normally Advocates Depute, Crown counsel in the High court, and the procurator fiscal or a Depute in the sheriff court. At the close of the prosecution's evidence, the defence may submit that in law there is no case to answer. If this plea is upheld, the accused will be acquitted. Otherwise guilt or innocence is determined by the jury sworn to try the case.

In considering their verdict the jury may decide to find the accused 'guilty', 'not guilty' or 'not proven'. The verdict may be reached by a simple majority but a guilty verdict can only be reached if at least eight of the jury are in favour of it. The size of the majority is not disclosed.

There is no practical difference in effect between a verdict of not guilty and one of not proven; both are acquittals and have the effect that the accused cannot be tried again for the same offence.

In *summary procedure* the main difference is that trial is not by jury. The proceedings at the trial, broadly speaking, follow the pattern of a trial by solemn procedure, which includes the possibility of the accused person raising a plea of 'no case to answer' at the close of evidence for the prosecution.

Extradition
Scotland is covered by Britain's extradition arrangements with a large number of countries (see p. 34).

Civil Judicial Procedure
Civil litigation in Scottish courts takes the form of adversary procedure. In other words, the court decides a case on the basis of the facts alleged and proved by the litigants or their lawyers and on their legal arguments.

Actions in the Court of Session

An action in the Court of Session begins when one litigant, the pursuer, serves a summons (frequently by post) on the other litigant, the defender. The summons is duly registered and signeted in the offices of court. (The signet is a seal by which certain writs in the name of the Sovereign, including a Court of Session summons, are authenticated.) The summons normally warns the defender that if he or she does not appear before the court and defend the action, the court will grant a decree in his or her absence in favour of the pursuer. A request to the court to grant the remedy sought by the pursuer, called the conclusion of the summons, is attached to the summons. A detailed statement of the facts upon which the pursuer relies, called the condescendence, is also attached. There is also a brief statement of the legal grounds, called the pleas-in-law, which, if the facts are proved, would entitle the pursuer to the remedy he or she seeks.

The defender has a chance to put forward a statement of the facts, either accepting or rejecting the pursuer's statement, together with the pleas-in-law in support of the argument. Both pursuer and defender are subsequently given an opportunity to adjust their own cases in the light of the statements and allegations put forward by the other side. The object of these written pleadings is to focus on the area of disagreement between the litigants and to give each party fair notice of the case to be answered.

The pleadings are then made into a 'closed record', which sets out, one against the other, the numbered allegations, admissions and denials of each party. The matter goes forward for determination by the court. If the dispute concerns questions of law, then the court will hear a debate between counsel on those legal questions and, if the parties agree about the facts, the court will then issue its decision. This will usually either grant or refuse the remedy sought by the pursuer. If there is a dispute over the facts the evidence is considered by a judge sitting alone without a jury, or, in certain matters—usually damages actions—before the judge sitting with a jury. In civil matters, the jury has 12 members.

Petitions in the Court of Session

Petitions are the other common form of judicial proceedings. A petition is strictly an *ex parte* application to the court (an application made, or in the interests of, one side only, or made by a person who has an interest in proceedings but is not party to them). Petitions are often used where the petitioner and the respondents to the petition are not in dispute but where the court's approval for some matter is nevertheless required by law. Examples include petitions for:

—the sequestration of an insolvent person;

—the liquidation of a company;

—an order enabling a person to adopt a child;

—the appointment of a judicial factor to administer property; and

—the variation of trust purposes.

Some types of petition—such as petitions for the custody of children—are often contentious. A petition is presented to the court, and the court then decides who should be served with, or made aware of, the petition. Any respondent to the petition may lodge answers in much the same way as any defender to a summons can lodge defences.

Sheriff Court Civil Procedure

The sheriff court has a tripartite procedural system consisting of:

—ordinary actions (commenced by initial writ);

—summary cause actions (commenced by summons) and small claims actions; and

—summary and other special applications (also commenced by initial writ).

As 'actions', the first two categories correspond broadly to Court of Session actions, and are raised by the pursuer to enforce or protect his or her legal rights or to ensure that the defender carries out his or her legal obligation.

The object of a sheriff court summary application, which resembles a Court of Session petition, is to obtain from the sheriff power to do something or to require something to be done for which the sheriff's authority is needed. This is usually a matter of statute law but in a few cases it is a matter of common law. In such applications the sheriff disposes of a wide variety of administrative and other matters. The procedure in a summary application is at the sheriff's discretion and this distinguishes summary applications from special applications; in such cases, the procedure is wholly or partly prescribed by statute or act of sederunt. Summary causes are relatively quick, simple and cheap. A summary cause action may be raised or defended by an ordinary citizen (for example, to recover consumer debts) but the procedure is also extensively used by trading and commercial organisations and by local authorities. It is much easier for a person to act without legal representation in summary causes than in ordinary actions or summary applications.

A small claims procedure was introduced in 1988 for claims not exceeding £750. The small claims procedure has a number of features which are not available in summary cause procedure and which seek to enable the individual to pursue or defend a claim without legal representation. These include service to the summons by the sheriff clerk, easy-to-complete forms, and an upper limit of £75 on expenses.

International Convention on Civil Jurisdiction and Enforcement of Judgments

Scotland, like England and Wales, is covered by the Brussels Convention on Civil Jurisdiction and Enforcement of Judgments (see p. 37).

The Personnel of the Legal System

The personnel of the law includes the judges and the members of the legal profession, the advocates and solicitors. It also includes others who administer the legal system. In the central and local courts, for example, these include the clerks of the courts (such as the sheriff clerks, whose office dates from the earliest times), and their subordinate officials.

Judges

In Scotland far greater use is made of full-time legally qualified judges than in England (where lay magistrates play a greater role). Nevertheless, many prosecutions are dealt with by the lay summary courts. As in England and Wales, professional judges in Scotland are drawn from legal practitioners rather than from people specially trained to be judges throughout their career—in contrast to the general practice in many other parts of Europe.

Since the Court of Session and the sheriff courts are the Queen's courts, all judicial appointments in these courts are made by the Sovereign, acting on the advice of Government Ministers.

The Prime Minister makes recommendations for the appointment of the Lord President and the Lord Justice-Clerk, and also the two Scottish judges in the House of Lords. The Secretary of State for Scotland makes recommendations for the other judicial appointments. By tradition these ministers consult the Lord Advocate before making their recommendations.

The judges of the Court of Session are appointed from among senior advocates. Many have already gained experience as sheriffs principal. Sheriffs principal, full-time judges resident in their sheriffdom, are next in the judicial hierarchy. Only people who have been qualified as an advocate or solicitor for ten years are eligible for appointment as sheriffs principal or as sheriffs (the next rank in the hierarchy). In the past sheriffs were usually appointed from among advocates, but currently as many solicitors as advocates are being appointed.

The holding of judicial office is prescribed by age. Since 1959 all Court of Session judges have had a retirement age of 75; all sheriffs principal and sheriffs appointed since 1961 have a retiring age of 72. A sheriff principal or sheriff below retirement age can only be removed from office by the Secretary of State for Scotland, who acts on the advice of the Lord President and Lord Justice-Clerk following an inquiry into his or her fitness for office. An order for removal must be made by statutory instrument which is laid before each House of Parliament for negative resolution. There is no comparable procedure for the removal of a judge of the Court of Session.

District Courts

In the district court, ordinary citizens, rather than legally qualified full-time judges, sit on the bench. Provision is also made for district or islands councils to appoint stipendiary magistrates although at present only Glasgow has done so. The lay judges of the district courts are all justices of the peace. Most are appointed justices by the Secretary of State acting on behalf of the Queen. Others are nominated by local authorities; district and islands councils may appoint up to one quarter of their members to be ex officio justices. Stipendiary magistrates must have been advocates or solicitors for at least five years before appointment.

The Legal Profession

Advocates

Advocates correspond to barristers elsewhere in Britain. All advocates are members of the Faculty of Advocates which is also the governing body of the Scottish Bar. Although solicitors can appear in courts, the expression 'the Scottish Bar' usually denotes only advocates. The elected Dean of Faculty and his or her Council control the discipline of advocates. Until 1991 advocates had an exclusive right of audience in the High Court of Justiciary and the Court of Session (This right has now been extended to solicitors—see below). They can appear in every other court in Scotland and have the same right as English barristers to appear before the House of Lords, the Privy Council and Parliamentary Committees.

Solicitors

Some of the work done by solicitors is currently under review. They undertake most of the litigation in the sheriff courts but, until 1991, did not have a right of audience in the supreme civil or criminal courts. The Law Reform (Miscellaneous Provisions) (Scotland) Act 1990 extended rights of audience in the high courts to solicitors. Solicitors have the exclusive right to act as agent in conveying land for clients although the 1990 Act also provided for a new profession of qualified conveyancer to be established. Solicitors have hitherto had the exclusive right to brief advocates in litigation. The Faculty is, however, now prepared to accept briefs direct from a limited number of professional organisations. Solicitors also discharge many kinds of business over which they have no statutory monopoly—such as negotiations for the sale or purchase of land, estate management and management of trusts and executries, and advice on financial, commercial and fiscal problems.

All practising solicitors must be members of the Law Society of Scotland, the statutory governing body of Scottish solicitors. The Society's functions include:

—regulating solicitors' fees;

—representing solicitors in their relations with government, other bodies and the public;

—making representations for law reform;

—enforcing standards of professional conduct; and

—maintaining a guarantee fund out of which payments are made to people who have suffered financial loss through dishonesty on the part of any solicitor in practice.

Professional Bodies

The Faculty of Advocates and the Law Society of Scotland have their own professional examinations. Professional advocates or solicitors usually obtain exemption from these by including the necessary professional subjects in a law degree from a Scottish University and obtaining a diploma in legal practice. The prospective advocate must then undergo training in a solicitor's office followed by training under a practising advocate (called pupillage, or sometimes 'devilling'). During this period he or she must take Faculty of Advocates examinations in certain practical subjects for which a degree gives no exemption. Solicitors wishing to practise on their own account or in a partnership of solicitors must every year take out a practising certificate from the Law Society of Scotland which maintains the Roll of Solicitors.

Messengers-at-arms and Sheriff Officers

In contrast to the position in England, the functions of collecting sums due under decrees of the Scottish courts, and of enforcing debts due under court decrees in the event of the debtor's failure to pay, are not discharged by the courts and their full-time officials. After granting a decree, a Scottish court will leave the successful party to obtain payment or secure performance. If that fails, the successful party (or his or her solicitor) must instruct a messenger-at-arms or sheriff officer to enforce the decree. Sheriff court decrees are enforced by sheriff officers and Court of Session decrees by messengers-at-arms or, in a sheriffdom which has no messengers, by a sheriff officer.

Messengers-at-arms are appointed and disciplined by the Lord Lyon King of Arms. Sheriff officers are granted commissions from and are disciplined by the appropriate sheriff principal. Messengers and sheriff officers charge fees which are prescribed by rules made by the Court of Session. Like solicitors, they may be in business on their own account or in partnerships. They can be employed under a contract of service by another officer or by a firm of officers but the terms of their commission cannot tie them to a particular employer. An officer may not form a private or public company for the purpose of exercising his or her official functions nor can he or she exercise any official functions as an employee of such a company.

Administration of the Scottish Legal System

Courts' Administration
Responsibility for organising and administering the supreme and sheriff courts is shared by the courts themselves and by the Secretary of State for Scotland, a Cabinet Minister. The Supreme Courts, the Court of Session and the High Court of Justiciary enact the rules regulating their own procedure and the procedures of the sheriff court and the lay summary courts. The Statutory Rules Council and Sheriff Court Rules Council, consisting of judges and legal practitioners, advise the Supreme Courts of amendments of the rules. The Secretary of State's responsibility for the organisation and administration of the sheriff courts and, to a lesser extent, the Supreme Courts is carried out by the Scottish Courts Administration: it deals with such non-legal, practical matters as the accommodation and staffing of the courts and the pay and conditions of service of the clerks of court and the other officers who assist in the proper running of the courts.

District and islands councils, advised by justices' committees, administer the district courts, providing them with, for example, buildings and clerks of court. The justices' committees approve the duty rota of justices and administer training schemes for justices made by the Secretary of State for Scotland. Judges, whether lay or professional, are not in any way subject to ministerial control and the independence of the courts is scrupulously observed. The Lord Advocate has limited functions in relation to some civil proceedings and is, for example, responsible for the procedural rules for the Lands Tribunal for Scotland.

Ministerial Supervision

The Secretary of State for Scotland, through the Scottish Courts Administration, appoints the staff of the High Court of Justiciary and the Court of Session, and is responsible for the composition, staffing and organisation of the sheriff courts. District courts are staffed and administered by the district and islands local authorities.

The Secretary of State is also responsible for the criminal law of Scotland, crime prevention, the police, the penal system, and legal aid; he or she is advised on parole matters by the Parole Board for Scotland.

The Lord Advocate and the Solicitor General for Scotland are the chief legal advisers to the Government on Scottish questions and the principal representatives of the Crown for the purposes of litigation in Scotland. The Lord Advocate is closely concerned with legal policy and administration. He or she must exercise an independent discretion when prosecuting crime.

Different ministers are responsible to Parliament for keeping under review the various branches of the law of Scotland and for sponsoring Bills for law reform. Some important branches of law are the responsibility of ministers for the whole of Britain. The President of the Board of Trade (Secretary of State for Trade and Industry) is answerable to Parliament for overseeing large parts of Scottish mercantile and commercial law. In general, however, most branches of the law are the responsibility of the Scottish departments. Thus, the Lord Advocate has ministerial responsibility for the law relating to the jurisdiction and procedure of Scottish courts in civil (but not criminal) proceedings and certain other matters: the responsibility is discharged through the Scottish Courts Administration in Edinburgh.

The Lord Advocate is also in charge of the Lord Advocate's Department in London which includes the Scottish Parliamentary Counsel (who draft Scottish legislation sponsored by any government department). The Secretary of State for Scotland is responsible generally for all branches of Scots law not allocated to other ministers including, for example, criminal law and procedure, family law, the law of succession, and land tenure.

Agencies of Law Reform
The Lord Advocate appoints the members of the Scottish Law Commission and approves their programmes of law reform. The Commission is a permanent statutory body, consisting of five lawyers of high repute, which has the duty of keeping the whole law of Scotland under review with a view to its systematic development and reform. Proposals for law reform are made in the form of published reports, often with draft legislation in the annexes which may be introduced either by ministers or ordinary MPs.

Justice Charter
The Justice Charter, part of the Citizen's Charter initiative, sets out a number of commitments to improve procedures, information and facilities for people using the Scottish courts.

The Courts and the Executive

The control exercised by the courts over public authorities is primarily intended to ensure that they keep within the limits of their powers and do not act *ultra vires*, or beyond their legal power and authority.

The more important legal remedies in such cases are decrees of *declarator, reduction, interdict, specific implement* and *damages*. All are available in actions between private persons. Scottish civil procedure enables all or any of the remedies to be obtained in a single action.

Declarator

The object of a decree of declarator is to establish or vindicate some legally enforceable right of the pursuer. The decree may establish this right either directly, by declaring that the pursuer has the right, or indirectly, for example, by declaring that the defender has no competing right. Unlike other remedies, a declarator does not order something to be done or prevent something from being done; it merely declares the particular state of affairs. It may be obtained before some action is taken by a public authority, to ensure that some right of the pursuer is taken into account by that authority. However, the decree may be refused if an alternative remedy exists or if there is no actual dispute between the parties.

Reduction

Reduction is essentially a negative remedy by which the whole or any part of an act of a public authority may be reduced (that is, annulled or set aside) on the grounds that the authority has acted *ultra vires*. An action of reduction may only be brought in the Court of Session, and must be commenced within 20 years of the *ultra vires* act. However, the court may refuse the remedy if there was delay in bringing the action. Its availability may be restricted by the statute under which the public authority is acting. The remedy may also be refused if lesser remedies would suffice.

Interdict

An interdict is a preventive remedy by which a person may protect his or her rights when they are threatened by the proposed wrongful actions of a public authority. The decree prohibits the authority from infringing the rights in question. It may be refused where there is an alternative remedy such as a statutory penalty. Interdict is not available against the Crown. Unlike reduction and declarator, however, the court may grant an interim interdict to maintain the status quo pending the court's final decision.

Specific Implement

The Court of Session has the power to order a public authority, other than the Crown, to perform a statutory duty by making an order for 'specific implement'. The court may also prescribe such penalties (including fine and imprisonment) in the event of the order not being implemented as it considers to be appropriate. A person may obtain a decree of specific implement only if the duty of the authority is judicially enforceable and owed by the authority to that person. He or she cannot enforce the duty if it is owed to someone else or to the community as a whole.

Damages

A public authority is liable to make reparation (that is, compensation) for any damage which it causes through the negligent exercise of its statutory powers and duties. A person injured in this way may bring an action of damages against the authority to determine the authority's liability and the amount of compensation due and to obtain an order for payment.

Legal Aid

Both branches of the Scottish legal profession had a long history of giving free assistance to the poor involved in litigation. The machinery for giving this assistance was the *poor's roll* which stemmed from an Act of the Scottish Parliament of 1424. Today legal aid is paid for by the state on a similar basis to the system in England and Wales (see p. 58) and since 1987 has been adminis- tered by the Scottish Legal Aid Board.

The Legal System of Northern Ireland

Northern Ireland's legal system is in many ways similar to that in England and Wales. The original Celtic laws of custom in Ireland remained uninfluenced by either English law or Roman law from continental Europe until quite late in the Middle Ages. From the end of the twelfth century, however, when King Henry II established a colony in the part of Ireland known as 'the Pale', English influence on Irish law and government became marked. By the year 1400 the pattern of the judicial system was firmly established along English lines, although courts offered justice only to the Anglo-Irish and most native Irishmen remained under Celtic law. It was, in fact, not until the seventeenth century that law on the English model applied throughout Ireland. The subsequent parallel development of English law and the law enforced in Northern Ireland courts has been assisted by the existence of a common court of appeal, the House of Lords in London.

Jury trials have the same place in the Northern Ireland legal system as in that of England and Wales, except in the case of offences involving acts of terrorism (see p. 100). In addition, the course of litigation is the same and the legal profession has the same two branches (see p. 54).

Parliament and Government

In 1801 the Irish Parliament joined that of Great Britain, establishing the United Kingdom. The arrangement lasted for over a century but in 1922 Southern Ireland (now the Irish Republic) became a self-governing country outside the United Kingdom. Meanwhile the Government of Ireland Act 1920 had enacted a constitution for Northern Ireland. This preserved the supreme authority of the United Kingdom Parliament in London and reserved certain matters to Westminster. At the same time Northern Ireland was provided with its own subordinate legislature and executive to deal with many domestic matters such as agriculture, commerce, development, education, health and social services. As a result, in many aspects of home affairs modern Northern Ireland legislation has a different source from corresponding English or Scottish statutes, and may differ in substance. The Northern Ireland Parliament had jurisdiction over all matters relating to the inferior courts, but all Supreme Court matters remained the responsibility of the British Parliament.

This system continued until 1972 when a period of direct rule by the British Government began. Northern Ireland continues to be governed by direct rule under legislation passed in 1974. This allows the Parliament in London to approve all laws for Northern Ireland and places its government departments under the direction and control of the Secretary of State for Northern Ireland, who is a Cabinet Minister.[13]

Superior Courts

The Supreme Court of Judicature comprises the Court of Appeal, the High Court and the Crown Court. All matters relating to these superior courts are under the jurisdiction of the British Parliament.

[13]For further details, see *The British System of Government* and *Northern Ireland* (Aspects of Britain: HMSO, 1992).

Judges are appointed by the Crown and can only be removed on an address from both Houses of Parliament.

The Court of Appeal comprises the Lord Chief Justice (as President) and two Lords Justices of Appeal. The High Court comprises the Lord Chief Justice and five other judges. The practice and procedure of the Court of Appeal and the High Court are virtually the same as in the corresponding courts in England and Wales. Both courts sit in the Royal Courts of Justice in Belfast.

The Court of Appeal has power to review the civil law decisions of the High Court and the criminal law decisions of the Crown Court, and may in certain cases review the decisions of county courts and magistrates' courts. Subject to certain restrictions, an appeal from a judgment of the Court of Appeal lies to the House of Lords.

The High Court is divided into a Queen's Bench Division, dealing with most civil law matters, and a Chancery Division, dealing with, for instance, trusts and estates, title to land, mortgages and charges, wills and company matters.

The Crown Court deals with all serious criminal cases.

Inferior Courts

The inferior courts in Northern Ireland are the county courts and the magistrates' courts, both of which differ in a number of ways from their counterparts in England and Wales.

County courts are primarily civil law courts. They are presided over by one of 12 county court judges, two of whom—in Belfast and Londonderry—have the title of recorder. Appeals lie from the county courts to the High Court. The county courts also deal with appeals from the magistrates' courts.

The general civil jurisdiction of the county courts includes the determination of most actions (not undefended divorce cases) in which the amount or the value of specific articles claimed is below a specified value. The courts also deal with actions involving title to or the recovery of land; equity matters such as trusts and estates; mortgages and the sale of land and partnerships.

The day-to-day work of dealing summarily with minor local criminal cases is carried out in each of the 22 'petty sessions' districts by *magistrates' courts* presided over by a resident magistrate—a paid judge with legal qualifications, similar to stipendiary magistrates in England and Wales. The magistrates' courts also exercise jurisdiction in certain family law cases and a very limited jurisdiction in other civil cases.

Terrorist Offences

People accused of offences specified under emergency legislation (called 'scheduled offences' which relate to terrorism) are tried in the Crown Court without jury. The onus remains on the prosecution to prove guilt beyond reasonable doubt and the defendant has the right to be represented by a lawyer of his or her choice. The judge must set out in a written statement the reasons for convicting and there is an automatic right of appeal to the Court of Appeal against conviction and sentence on points of fact as well as of law.

Administration of the Law

The administration and procedures of all criminal and civil courts are the responsibility of the Lord Chancellor, while the Northern Ireland Office, under the Secretary of State, deals with substantive criminal and civil law, the police and the penal system. The Lord

Chancellor has general responsibility for legal aid, advice and assistance.

The Director of Public Prosecutions for Northern Ireland, who is responsible to the Attorney General, prosecutes all offences tried on indictment, and may do so in other (summary) cases. Most summary offences are prosecuted by the police.

European Community Law

Britain has been a member of the European Community since 1973.[13] In certain circumstances, European Community law takes precedence over domestic law. It is normally applied by the domestic courts. The most authoritative rulings are given by the Community's *Court of Justice*, which consists of 13 judges, and adjudicates on the meaning of the treaties and on any measures taken by the Council of Ministers and the European Commission. It can, for instance, declare void an act of the Council or the Commission which infringes the treaties, or whose legality has been challenged by the Council, a member state, or an individual directly concerned. In addition, at the request of national courts, the Court gives a preliminary ruling on the interpretation or the validity of Community law. Its rulings must be applied in member states.

The Court also hears complaints and appeals brought by or against Community institutions, member states or individuals, and gives preliminary rulings on cases referred by courts in the member states. In practice, cases involving individuals are only likely to come before the Court as a result of a preliminary reference. It is the final authority on Community law and its rulings must be applied in member states.

The Court has 13 judges, including at least one from each member state, assisted by advocates-general. The latter make rea-

[13]For further details, see *Britain in the European Community* (Aspects of Britain: HMSO, 1992).

soned submissions in each case brought before the Court in order to assist it in its interpretation and application of Community law. This is done after the parties have completed their written and oral submissions. The Court is free to accept or reject the advocate-general's conclusions by applying a different line of reasoning.

There is also a *Court of First Instance*, which opened in 1989 and is intended to relieve the Court of Justice of some of its work-load. Twelve members sit in the Court, which has jurisdiction over staff cases, certain actions against a Community institution in relation to the Community's competition rules, and certain cases under the European Steel and Coal Community Treaty. The Court of First Instance has taken over some of the work previously done by the Court of Justice, thus enabling the latter to consider cases in its own jurisdiction within an acceptable period of time.

Community policies are implemented by a variety of means:

—regulations which are legally binding on all member states;

—directives which are binding on member states to which they are addressed but which allow national authorities to decide on methods of implementation;

—decisions which are binding on those to whom they are addressed such as member states, firms or individuals; and

—recommendations and opinions which have no binding force.

The Council of Ministers can also indicate a general policy direction through resolutions.

Appendix

The Police Service

There are 52 police forces in Britain (43 in England and Wales, 8 in Scotland and one in Northern Ireland), mainly organised on a local basis. The Metropolitan Police Force and the City of London force are responsible for policing London. At the end of 1991 police strength in Britain was just over 149,500, of which the Royal Ulster Constabulary numbered over 8,489. Each force has an attachment of volunteer special constables who perform police duties in their spare time, without pay, acting mainly as auxiliaries to the regular force. In Northern Ireland there is a 4,967-strong part-time and full-time paid reserve.

Policing in England and Wales is based on a tripartite structure of the Home Secretary, police authorities, and chief constables. Local administration for the police in each area is carried out by the police authority, two-thirds of whose members are local councillors and one-third magistrates. The police authority's general duty is to maintain an adequate and efficient police force for the area. The Home Secretary is directly accountable to Parliament for the Metropolitan Police. In Scotland, forces are maintained by regional and islands councils. The Police Authority for Northern Ireland is appointed by the Government.

Chief constables are in charge of their police forces and are responsible for the appointment, promotion and discipline of all ranks below assistant chief constable. They are generally answerable to the police authorities on matters of efficiency, and must submit an annual report.

The police authorities appoint the chief constable and other senior officers. They also fix the maximum permitted strength of the force and provide buildings and equipment. In the Metropolitan Police area the commissioner of police and his or her deputies are appointed on the recommendation of the Home Secretary.

The police service is financed by central and local government.

Central Control of the Police Service

The Home Secretary and the Secretaries of State for Scotland and Northern Ireland approve the appointment of chief, deputy and assistant chief constables. Where necessary they can:

—require a police authority to retire a chief constable in the interests of efficiency;

—call for a report from a chief constable on matters relating to local policing; and

—institute a local inquiry.

The same ministers can also make regulations covering the following:

—qualifications for appointment, promotion and retirement;

—discipline;

—hours of duty, leave, pay and allowances; and

—uniform.

All police forces (except the Metropolitan Police) are inspected by inspectors of constabulary reporting to central government.

On request, the inspectorate also undertakes inspections of selected parts of the Metropolitan Police.

Police Complaints Authority

The independent Police Complaints Authority, established under the Police and Criminal Evidence Act 1984, has powers to:

—supervise the investigation of serious complaints against any police officer in the 43 forces of England and Wales; and

—take the final decision on whether a police officer should be charged with a breach of discipline.

Addresses

Government Departments

Home Office, 50 Queen Anne's Gate, London SW1H 9AT.

Legal Secretariat to the Law Officers, Attorney General's Chambers, 9 Buckingham Gate, London SW1E 6JP.

Lord Advocate's Department, Fielden House, 10 Great College Street, London SW1P 3SL.

Lord Chancellor's Department, Trevelyan House, 30 Great Peter Street, London SW1P 2BY.

Northern Ireland Office, Whitehall, London SW1A 2AZ.

Scottish Office, New St Andrew's House, Edinburgh EH1 3SX.

Other Organisations

General Council of the Bar, 3 Bedford Row, London WC1R 4DB.

The Bar Council of Northern Ireland, Royal Courts of Justice, Chichester Street, Belfast BT1 3JY.

Criminal Law Revision Committee, c/o Home Office, Queen Anne's Gate, London SW1H 9AT.

Inn of Court of Northern Ireland, Royal Courts of Justice, Belfast BT1 3NX.

Justice (the British Section of the International Commission of Jurists), 95a Chancery Lane, London WC2A 2DT.

Law Commission, Conquest House, 37–38 John Street, Theobalds Road, London WC1N 2BQ.

Law Reform Committee, c/o Lord Chancellor's Department, Trevelyan House, 30 Great Peter Street, London SW1P 2BY.

The Law Society, 50 Chancery Lane, London WC2A 1SX.

Law Society of Northern Ireland, 90–106 Victoria Street, Belfast BT1 3JZ.

The Law Society of Scotland, 26–28 Drumsheugh Gardens, Edinburgh EH3 7YR.

Legal Aid Head Office, 5th & 6th Floors, 29/37 Red Lion Street, London WC1R 4PP.

National Council for Civil Liberties, 21 Tabard Street, London SE1 4LA.

Scottish Law Commission, 140 Causewayside, Edinburgh EH9 1PR.

Further Reading

			£
The British System of Government (Aspects of Britain)			
ISBN 0 11 701677 2	HMSO	1992	5.25
Criminal Justice (Aspects of Britain)			
ISBN 0 11 701692 6	HMSO	1992	5.00
Citizen's Charter			
ISBN 0 10 115992 7	HMSO	1991	8.50
The Courts Charter			
Lord Chancellor's Department	HMSO	1992	
A New Framework for Local Justice			
ISBN 0 10 118292 9	HMSO	1992	3.55
GELDART, William			
Introduction to English Law	Oxford		
ISBN 0 19 289221 5	University Press	1991	6.99
Human Rights (Aspects of Britain)			
ISBN 0 11 701665 9	HMSO	1992	6.00
Justice Charter for Scotland	HMSO	1991	
Northern Ireland (Aspects of Britain)			
ISBN 0 11 701699 3	HMSO	1992	5.25

Annual Reports

Civil Judicial Statistics	
(England and Wales)	HMSO
Crown Prosecution Service	HMSO

Judicial Statistics	HMSO
Law Commission	HMSO
Lord Chancellor's Department	
Court Service	HMSO

Index

A MONTHLY UPDATE

ASPECTS OF BRITAIN

Current Affairs
a monthly survey

September 1992   Vol 22   No 9

London Conference on Former Yugoslavia
Outcome of the EC/UN Peace Conference

Balance of Payments 1991
Balance of Payments 'Pink Book'

Iraq
Deployment of Allied Military Aircraft over Southern Iraq

Research and Development
The Government's Annual Review of R & D

Regional Trends
Analysis of Regional Contrasts in Britain

CURRENT AFFAIRS:
A MONTHLY SURVEY

Using the latest authoritative information from official and other sources, *Current Affairs* is an invaluable digest of important developments in all areas of British affairs. Focusing on policy initiatives and other topical issues, its factual approach makes it the ideal companion for *Britain Handbook* and *Aspects of Britain*. Separate sections deal with governmental; international; economic; and social, cultural and environmental affairs. A further section provides details of recent documentary sources for these areas. There is also a twice-yearly index.

Annual subscription including index and postage £35·80 net.
Binder £4·95.

Buyers of Britain 1993: An Official Handbook *qualify for a discount of 25 per cent on a year's subscription to* Current Affairs *(see next page).*

HMSO Publications Centre
(Mail and telephone orders only)
PO Box 276
LONDON SW8 5DT
Telephone orders: 071 873 9090

THE ANNUAL PICTURE

BRITAIN
1993

AN OFFICIAL HANDBOOK

BRITAIN HANDBOOK

The annual picture of Britain is provided by *Britain: An Official Handbook* - the forty-fourth edition will be published early in 1993. It is the unrivalled reference book about Britain, packed with information and statistics on every facet of British life.

With a circulation of over 20,000 worldwide, it is essential for libraries, educational institutions, business organisations and individuals needing easy access to reliable and up-to-date information, and is supported in this role by its sister publication, *Current Affairs: A Monthly Survey*.

Approx. 500 pages; 24 pages of colour illustrations; 16 maps; diagrams and tables throughout the text; and a statistical section. Price £19·50.

Buyers of Britain 1993: An Official Handbook *have the opportunity of a year's subscription to* Current Affairs *at 25 per cent off the published price of £35·80. They will also have the option of renewing their subscription next year at the same discount. Details in each copy of* Handbook, *from HMSO Publications Centre and at HMSO bookshops (see back of title page).*

Printed in the UK for HMSO.
Dd 0294518, 2/93, C30, 51-2432, 5673.